Profound Prayer

Profound Prayer

A Modern Prayer Guide for Peace, Power, and Personal Transformation

Christopher Lepine

Soulscape Publishing

Profound Prayer

A Modern Prayer Guide for Peace, Power, and
Personal Transformation

By
Christopher Lepine

Published by:

Soulscape Publishing
P.O. Box 156
Newark, DE 19715

First edition 2022

Library of Congress Control Number: 2020902944
ISBN: 978-0-9634081-5-0

To my dear God, whose Spirit within guides me
each day and nourishes my soul.

Contents

Part III: Unlimited Transformation

We think we must climb to a certain height of goodness before we can reach God. But . . . if we are in a hole the Way begins in the hole. The moment we set our face in the same direction as His, we are walking with God.

—Helen Wodehouse, *Inner Light*

Introduction

The Doorway to Help

Our souls are hurting and hungry—some starving. The digitally-infused world is sucking life from our spiritual selves: It wants our eyes, ears, fingers, and minds. It wants all our time and attention.

We're continually attacked by the incessant attention seeking of smartphones, tablets, computers, and countless other digital pests as well as the disruptions and changes that they bring to the world. Sure, we can set limits, but today's remarkably complex and hyper-accelerated modern civilizations have a tendency to separate us from each other and from God.

Today, more than ever, we need the power of profound prayer to nourish our souls so we can adapt and thrive and make a positive difference. We need the infinite power of our Divine Parent, the very Creator of our souls.

This book will show you how to get that power each day: You'll be the master of your digital life and the modern world, not their slave. You'll be better able to give the proper time and attention to every aspect of your life. The digital world will still remain a critical part of your life but not the main focus.

You'll learn to nourish your soul to give you strength for the transformation that you need. Leading a meaningful, principled, and positive life takes real energy, and that comes from your soul. *The key is to keep your spiritual batteries charged—supercharged—*while you work hard to do good and remake yourself.

There is no other way.

Please come with an open mind and a willingness to explore beyond what you know and assume. You might need to be a little uncomfortable at times . . . But, it will be worth it. Trust God's spirit to tell you what is true.

You're a child of God and have a birthright to an endless life of meaning, satisfaction, and unlimited personal growth. It's time to stretch beyond church, groups, or any limits to knowing God *directly*. It's time to immerse your soul in total contact with the divine spirit of God within. It's time for an unfiltered friendship and adventure with the true God.

It's time to unplug.

It's time for profound prayer.

Prayer is the doorway to all. It's the most effective and important personal growth technique and actually enlarges your capacity for God. Nothing has more growth impact. When in doubt, pray. When thankful, pray. Pray for others and yourself. If angry, pray. If bursting with joy, pray. No matter what problem or success, you can dive into divine dialogue to improve your thinking, embrace God's personal spirit within, and make timely, lasting, and effective decisions.

The doorway to problem-solving and achieving your goals is the most basic of activities—talking to God, exchanging your thoughts for God's: prayer. Prayer affects your *entire* being and is God's way of eternalizing you and satisfying your drives for completion, attainment, and liberation.

This book will show you how.

If you believe in God, you pray. When we pray, we all hope for divine help and yearn for answers to our most profound and pressing questions. We don't want a middleman: You probably don't want someone telling you what to do or setting up rules to control your access to or destiny with God.

Prayer is your birthright as a child of the Creator. Prayer—the truest prayer—is a direct communication with God that unlocks the endless storehouse of powerful divine gifts and personal transformation. If you want this experience, you have to build in daily, *uninterrupted* time for profound prayer and divine immersion. You also need to go beyond any tradition, group, church, or teaching that tries to control you or impose unfair human rules.

You have to find God yourself and develop a true friendship with the Creator. And, to do this, you need to rely on the secrets of effective, transforming, and energizing prayer; you need regular, direct contact with God to thrive in today's world.

You need to nourish your soul.

This book tells you exactly how to get that transforming, electrifying power. You'll learn how to find and talk to God through the secrets of effective prayer. You'll learn how to get the peace, hope, strength, and answers you need to live the adventure of your life while facing the ever-changing, very challenging world.

This book will give you each of the secrets of effective prayer with examples and discussions you can relate to. These principles and methods can lead you to the realization of a life *beyond your experience and imagination.* You can find unlimited satisfaction, spiritual success, joy, peace, confidence, progress, and happiness. And, you can lead the way for transformation of your family, friends, and others.

Prayer and divine immersion are the essential ingredients to make a better you and a better world. The secret of transforming the world is in transforming each and every person. It's the only way; nothing else works.

World Crisis

It's pretty plain that things aren't going well in the world. The old foundations of church and traditional beliefs are quickly eroding in the face of our unbalanced evolution with scientific and technological achievement. The fundamentals we relied on in the past cannot adapt quickly enough to help us manage our new, bewildering world: Limited philosophies and religions that used to work are left behind as people look for new directions and sources.

Since we're seeking for power and guidance to make the world a better place, we need real spiritual nourishment. But the vast majority of us remain in excruciating confusion and dissatisfaction: Many people don't even know where or how to fill the hunger or even what to call it.

But, there's great hope. More and more truth-seekers from inside and outside of religions are striving to get back to the most essential of human experiences—immersion in the Divine, friendship with God. We're about to rediscover the real universal spiritual truths that have always been there for the sincere, yearning, seekers of truth, givers of kindness, and servants to others—the faith children of God.

This book is based on those stunning universal truths and reveals the principles and techniques of divine immersion—the practice of ideal profound prayer.

The Universal Spiritual Way

Now it's time for you, me, and all humankind to work hard to create a future of peace, prosperity, and achievement for all people. It's time for us to enthusiastically embrace and fearlessly live The Universal Spiritual Way—the original teachings of Jesus.

You're a child of a perfect Divine Parent who is a person you can know, and all are your sisters and brothers united through this heritage. You weren't born with sin on your soul: *Jesus never taught this.* The ticket to an eternal life is to wholeheartedly try to find and follow your inner guidance from The Universal Father.

I'll often refer to God as a Father throughout this book since I'm talking about the first person of the trinity of God the Father, God the Son, and God the Spirit. God doesn't have gender, but God the Father loves *as a father.* God is not male or female, but the best way to understand God the Father is as a perfect divine deity that is the source of the best father-love found in the best human parents.

This book focuses mainly on the central role that God the Father has in nourishing/supercharging our souls through a piece of himself that is different in each of us—the inner spirit of God. God the Father, God the Son, and God the Spirit are equal, but this book looks at the special role that God the Father has in our spiritual lives.

With our Divine Father's guidance, we'll strive to overcome all limitations and make great progress individually and collectively. We'll strive to transform the world and enjoy unending spiritual victory. We'll know deep friendships and be partners of God, creating truth, beauty, and goodness. It's what God wants for us; *it's what we were made for.*

You can know true happiness now and work toward an eternal life if you open up to the truth of your divine birthright. Prayer is the starting point. Prayer is the foundation of ascension and cosmic joy in The Universal Spiritual Way. The right kind of praying for yourself and others enables you to forget yourself when necessary or cry for help without fear or shame. You can achieve this self-transcending life if you're *wholeheartedly* sincere, hunger for the truth, and have the faith to follow God's guidance.

While everyone who responds to God's spirit from their heart is resurrected, *belief in the universal spiritual truths of The Universal Spiritual Way begins a real relationship with God the person* and spiritual growth *now.* Accepting and striving for these truths leads us to understand, forgive, and serve others, and achieve growth and world transformation—one person at a time.

But, transforming ourselves and the world is totally dependent on fully believing the essential universal spiritual truths and dedicating our lives to the Creator's will—love. Belief is a lens which can reveal new opportunity and possibility only if it's used, cleaned, and *changed* when inadequate or distorted. The core truths of The Universal Spiritual Way will never change, but our understanding of how to *live* them will change to keep pace with the evolution of humankind.

We'll always be perfecting our living of the golden rule—do unto to others as you would have them do unto you.

This Universal Spiritual Way unites humankind and propels us to a truly bright future. It's time to transcend the swamp of fear, anxiety, and doubt, to fly as the Creator's faith-children, joyfully working for spiritual success. Let's know family joy, community awareness, educational vision, industrial service and ethics, national purpose and vision, cultural and racial understanding, government effectiveness, fair international economic policy, the guarantee of worldwide peace and health, responsible environmental custody, and planetary unity.

Only belief and dedication to the universal spiritual truths will get us there. And, only prayer will give us the peace, assurance, security, hope, faith, confidence, and power to live such an invigorating, meaningful life based on following God's guidance: We need to nourish our souls every day.

About This Book

Profound Prayer is based on my decades of experience with the universal spiritual truths of The Universal Spiritual Way. The purpose of this book is to help you get the spiritual power and answers you need to face the challenges of your life and increase your spiritual growth. This book gives you the forgotten ancient wisdom of how to have a conversation with

God and nurture a divine friendship beyond the limits of church or group.

Please understand that I come as an *equal* in the spiritual search, a humble man who's known the pains, joys, and satisfactions of life, and sincerely desires growth and love. I firmly believe that the prayer and divine immersion techniques in this book are an ideal way to know God and totally energize our lives with hopeful purpose, confidence, courage, and self-forgetful service to others. It's my understanding of and attempt to live the spiritual truths in *The Urantia Book* that provides the foundation of my book.

Chapter 1, "The Breath of the Soul," introduces a prayer definition and summarizes its breadth and landscape. Next, Chapter 2, "Nourishment for Your Soul," defines the nature of the soul and how to feed it. Chapter 3, "The Incredible Power of Prayer," explores the amazing and unmatched power of prayer, followed next by Chapter 4, "How to Pray," which outlines the basic principles of true prayer along with a general approach for you to talk to God.

Chapter 5, "Prayer Killers," lists erroneous concepts and attitudes and how these impair or eliminate your God-reception. Chapter 6, "Prayer Answers," outlines principles of God's response and how these affect your approach to life and prayer. Chapter 7, "Prayer in Action," shares a series of beautiful, inspiring prayers. Chapter 8, "A Prayer Jump-Start," summarizes the basic prayer concepts of previous chapters and gives you clear steps and guidelines to pray. And, finally, Chapter 9, "Ideal Prayer," describes perfect prayer and what it will lead you to—the ultimate spiritual experience of divine immersion and a joyous life.

You'll see that the most critical concepts and techniques in this book are always repeated and are your roadmaps and touchstones. The keys of The Universal Spiritual Way and profound prayer are unforgettable as you see them woven into many contexts: (1) you have personal fellowship with the Creator, (2) you have value and uniqueness; you are irreplaceable, (3) you can overcome all limitations by faith, (4) your will/choice determines your inner experience and realization of your destiny (5) service to others is the supreme joy in life.

Those five keys that Jesus taught reveal the new spiritual landscape and provide the pathways to progress on earth and in life after death. This five-part foundation is the hidden secret of the most beneficial beliefs and methods of science, philosophy, and religion, and influences every progressive activity, group, and institution of our culture. It can also be the unbreakable foundation of *your* life. And, when you nourish yourself with ideal, profound prayer, when you get supercharged, you not only transform yourself, but your world.

So, please come with an open mind and fresh heart to explore the calming shores and inspiring summits of real prayer. Contemplate your divine kinship and friendship with God. The power, love, and revelation of your life's meaning and direction is in God's mind, waiting to flash to yours.

It's up to you. It's time to *feel* the Creator's unlimited love and the invigoration of the spirit within. Whatever your background, situation, job, or state of mind, if you come with an open mind and desire to learn, you'll know and expand the greatest experience of life—friendship with God.

Join me now. Discover your true, inner home. Discover endless profound power and transformation.

Part I

The Nature of Prayer

Prayer is . . . the sanctification of the soul, the foretaste of future blessedness, the angelic bliss, the heavenly rain, refreshing, watering, and fertilizing the ground of the soul, the power and strength of the soul and body, the purifying and freshening of the mental air, the enlightenment of the countenance, the joy of the spirit, the golden link, uniting the creature to the Creator.

—John Sergieff of Kronstadt, *My Life With Christ*

The Breath of the Soul

The Voice of the Real You

Chapter 1

Children are God's most beautiful creatures, and their growth in a healthy parental relationship is remarkable. They immediately trust and tap into great power and comfort. The love of a kind and wise father and mother provides a matchless foundation for a happy, confident, and successful life.

One of the most striking examples is children adopted from foreign countries, such as China. In most cases, potential parents arrive a day or two in China before they meet their child-to-be. The country is usually a completely new swirl of places, people, sounds, food, and countless everyday things as well as the logistics and paperwork of adoption. But, the children to be adopted will need to make much more challenging adaptations.

These new sons and daughters leave the only caregivers they can remember to be placed in the arms of new people with different faces, languages, customs, smells, foods, homes, communities, and cultures. And these children are usually too young to understand what's happening, only that it's radically different.

But, with good parents, children soon respond to affection and nurturing and give *absolute trust*: They accept their new lives and transform themselves. This most profound of trusts is the essential foundation to explore their new world and continue the adventure of life. They know they can talk to their parents about anything.

When we trust God and pray with faith, we're just like these children. Our souls are energized and nourished. We're empowered to live the wonderful destiny that God gives each of us.

Nearly all of us at some point have a strong desire to pray. Some pray every day, and others less often. Even though praying is a universal experience, most people don't understand or use it well; most of us ask for divine help but don't comprehend its scope or value. If we'd stop to reflect on the significance and benefits of daily divine contact, we'd soon want to get it right and do it more.

When you reach to God with all your heart, you often enter an *altered*, profound state that consistently brings the benefits you crave for your mind, body, and soul: No other activity can have such a lasting and important effect. We are truly *transformed* when we act on the truth that we're children of God and can become like Him.

We're supercharged.

The Spiritual Adventure and Our Need

It's almost too fantastic to comprehend: We start as simple animals in a vast universe and can actually make choices that bring us in contact with the very Being who's the source and upholder of creation. Our experiences and many opportunities for decision become the pageant of human freewill projected over the stretch and depth of a limitless adventure. We're given the supreme gift—life—to shine, jump, yell, play, struggle, succeed, and pray.

Prayer is the key, but for us to improve our prayer lives, we need to have a pretty deep and meaningful discussion. To unlock the secrets of profound prayer, you may have to expand your understanding of yourself. **So, stay with me with an open mind.** You may need to have a more complete understanding of how you're built. Here we go . . .

Your core is self-consciousness and free will; you know that you exist and are free to make decisions. These choices use and organize your gifts and resources and bring many outcomes in your life. Sit in a chair. Taste a food. Think about wildflowers. Watch a movie. Pray to God. You're making a choice. You've made decisions to do *something* and you know that you're alive and have the power of choice.

Just thinking and hoping for something to happen doesn't make it happen. You must do something. *Prayer is not a substitute for focus, hard work, and determination.* Visualize all you want, but you have to bring that vision to life with your own hands amidst real challenges. But, you probably already knew that! What you may not realize is that trying to follow God's instructions is a spiritual exertion for your soul that drains spiritual energy.

Prayer can lead us to that divine immersion that gives unlimited amounts of positive energy, enabling us to transform our minds and actions each day.

We're different and blessed from all other animals and life on earth. Our self-consciousness enables us to swim the invigorating and nourishing stream of people: a wild joke, a gliding dance step, a firm handshake, the enduring caress, a child's poetry, a good conversation, comforting understanding, and endless other joys. These are only possible with *people*. And, each of us is a person because we have a distinct personality—the unique gift of the Creator—and have the ability and liberation of using our other gifts of mind, body, and soul.

Relationships are *ends in themselves*. And, the greatest relationship we can have is with God. It all starts with prayer. It all starts with choice. It all starts with the power of our unique selves—our personalities.

Your unique freewill-personality allows you to move through space, touch and change objects, be expressive, contact people and find personal relationships, and approach God; we experience meaning, fact, and value, and make choices through the basic unity of the mind and its symbols (pictures) of the world.

We feel the impact of God's love and see eternal insights through the benefit of His Spirit within. These matchless and sublime experiences are only available to a person who knows she's a person and is able to make *decisions* based on the experience of the inner self and outer world of humanity.

When we make choices to respond to the divine within, when we follow God's lead, we collaborate with God to create a new part of ourselves: the soul. Your soul is a real thing and expresses your spiritual longings and relays spiritual realities within. It dramatically increases our spiritual capacity and power and can be the ticket to eternal life.

> The soul is the self-reflective, truth-discerning, and spirit-perceiving part of man which forever elevates the human being above the level of the animal world . . . the soul is that part of man which represents the potential survival value of human experience.
>
> —Jesus, from *The Urantia Book*

God unifies us with the ever-present need to satisfy spiritual urges and desires. He gives us the hunger to realize personal growth in all areas: This leads us to bring all parts of self to bear in a coordinated effort to find and become the best. It is perfection-hunger. But, along with self-consciousness is the profound need for stability, peace, and security when meeting needs and responding to danger.

Prayer is the first step in building the matchless foundation we desperately need. True prayer is the expression of the truest longings of your soul. True prayer brings real power to match real challenges to do the impossible.

The world bursts with stinging, real risks and profound uncertainties that can instantly crush human life or make it agonizing and fruitless. We all face the challenges of life but should take heart because God designed them to lead us to Him, beyond the confines of eye to the breathtaking plateaus of spiritual vision and reward.

> The pursuit of perfection, then, is the pursuit of sweetness and light. He who works for sweetness and light, works to make reason and the will of God prevail.
>
> —Matthew Arnold, *Culture and Anarchy*

This hunger for perfection produces great tension between the seen and the unseen: We can only be comforted by spiritual assurance and divine security. And that begins with prayer. And the more we pray, the greater our capacity to receive spiritual power.

While we live with real, and many times unavoidable dangers, our kind Divine Parent always provides the balm that meets all fear, anxiety, and need: He gives total peace and comfort and certainty. No matter what happens—damage to body, mind, family, or possessions—our souls are unhurt, always nourished, and truly invincible.

Every spiritual experience we had and worthy accomplishment is stored in the soul's memory: Our eternal lives begin with these treasures. After all, this is all we have after death. These joys encompass this and the next world but are only possible by the fact that we're children of God and a family unified in universe destiny by the Universal Father's will.

Aside from basic survival instincts, God plants the seeds that bring the real joys and accomplishments of life: We desire the satisfaction of self-expression, socialization, and success from personal expertise. These are the platform for higher spiritual satisfactions (our greatest needs) of service to others: love, personal improvement, and the hunger for truth.

By sincerely and wholeheartedly accepting our positive desires, urges, and experiences of the outer world and God, we realize the beginning of endless spiritual gifts and the invigorating, matchless motivation to know God and be like Him. This is our greatest need and the intense beacon that leads us through rolling waves to the portals of eternity and the calm harbors beyond. The overwhelming craving to touch God, to know and do His will through all decisions, leads to the perfect solution: prayer.

Prayer is the joyous, spontaneous, and stimulating expression of our souls. It nurtures and empowers, allowing the spiritual shift of perception and activity. The consequences of full heart expression to the Divine Father through the soul make prayer the perfect spiritual technique and lead to our most satisfying and edifying experience: We give thanks, tell God how much we adore and care for Him, and listen. We worship and commune.

Inner-worship of God is the gateway to all endless positive power and all spiritual gifts. Profound prayer, followed by sustained, selfless inner-worship of God, supercharges the soul.

By exercising the full realization of prayer and worship power, we can find solutions to all material and spiritual needs with complete assurance, security, peace, and accomplishment.

When we know and follow God, all things are possible. Those who reject contact with God live on the edge of the anxiety-fear cliff, never knowing if their needs will be met or life will go on. They have a constant burning, terrible hunger—a gigantic void.

But, people who accept and welcome divine assurance have an intense certainty that their most important needs are spiritual and will be met. Of course, they also realize that most of their non-spiritual needs will also be met. This liberation from the maze of animal survival gives you unending reserves of steady power and can lead to a life of meaningful, eternal achievements.

For instance, I could be a hair stylist at a local shop, concerned about work, yet anchored in spiritual prayer and worship peace. One day my manager comes over and says I'm just not turning over enough customers per day. My results, while very professional, have led to lower profits since I take the extra time. If I see this from an animal-survival stance, I'll act to guarantee survival at any cost, from reducing my customer time, to falsifying records—anything to avoid losing my job or coming up with a creative alternative.

But, since I come from a spiritual perspective, I talk to my boss and search for a solution that won't compromise my ideals but will keep me employed. Finally, I decide to change jobs because the boss wants profit first. Only through prayer am I certain that God will give me strength to find a better opportunity at a better shop, or a new career. The ability to go beyond the safe and materially-secure is born of spiritual certainty and assurance in the divine plan, which includes mortal growth and needs.

It all starts with conversations with God.

We're changed by our choices and the kind hand of God. Although we're fragile humans, we're cradled and caressed with our Father's kind touch and happy voice. Our Creator enables us to perform superhuman acts far transcending the survival instinct of an unthinking animal. Prayer is the perfect technique for meeting our needs and integrating our will with God's plan, of using our gifts to the fullest.

The Attitude Gateway

All spiritual progress really is possible but only if you form healthy attitudes: These determine how you express yourself in prayer and every choice you make. God won't interfere with your choices and will allow you to create any attitude, even the one that leads to self-destruction and soul death. With our focus on and understanding of choice-power, let's look at the ramifications of attitude on prayer.

Attitudes determine everything we'll experience inside ourselves and most of what we'll find in the outside world. Attitudes are orientations and tendencies toward things that touch our hearts, minds, souls, and bodies. God's incredible gift of freewill can bring life-giving revelations or it can grate on the dead surface of material survival, fear, selfishness, and hatred.

When you face the demands of life, please remember that your attitudes create roads that lead to or away from God; you're going forward or backward. Your attitude is a tool completely shaped by your will. You have total control; God will not interfere with your choices.

Attitudes are our reactions to experiences; they're the ways we've *decided* to consistently react. I think of four basic types: (1) *spiritually-progressive*, (2) *apathetic-lazy*, (3) *selfish*, or (4) *intentionally-destructive*.

If we're *spiritually-progressive*, we dedicate life to growth and God. We focus on spiritual things but are still practical about our material needs. Even though we get confused and might not know God's will, or misinterpret it and go against it, we've made an honest mistake and are spiritual. It's natural that we don't get it 100 percent right. God cares most about our true intentions. If we're *apathetic-lazy*, if we don't take time to engage in spiritual exercise or nourishment, if we avoid decisions, we're living as unconscious animals. We begin to think about only material things

When we're *selfish*, we know what the right and true way is (God's will) and decide to ignore it. We live selfishly; we sin.

When we're *intentionally-destructive*, we continually and unreservedly pursue defiance and rebellion against the divine will; we are iniquitous and soon kill our spiritual selves. We end any chance for a better life and an eternal existence. Our souls are starved to death—completely de-energized.

In reality, our lives are a mix of those different attitudes, hopefully evolving to an exclusively spiritually-progressive direction. God, of course, knows this and does all he can to help us find and respond to his light.

This spectrum of attitudes pervades every instant and life phase. It's based on our degree of knowledge of spiritual values and facts and willingness to do the Father's will. Our loving Parent has a perfect plan, which encircles all and brings the best throughout eternity.

When we vow to have an open and loving response to the Father's will, we act and become spiritual and transcend a sea of fear, anxiety, selfishness, and material-mindedness. Our animal evolutionary heritage has served as the foundation but was never intended as the final product of our relationship with God and others.

Even though many people choose selfishness and are even purposefully and wholeheartedly destructive, God incessantly pleads to their dark hearts. The Universal Father allows this free choice and is always hopeful that a person's attitude will change, so he can be responsive to spiritual rehabilitation. Patiently, with infinite understanding, our Creator yearns for our hearts to listen, look, and entwine with His Spirit to enter light and life.

God wants you to claim and live your birthright.

The breath of your soul—prayer—may be celebrated and used for praise and service or stifled and suffocated with the tangled web of apathy, selfishness, and rebellion against the Creator. While all other consequences and calamities may be overcome, if we purposefully reject the divine will and destroy our souls, there is no hope of resurrection and continued life after death: This condition is permanent. We no longer exist. We create the worst hell—non-existence.

These truths, while at many levels may make us a bit unsure, shouldn't cause fear or too much self-examination. God judges you by your *real* intentions, not your mistakes. He always gives you a chance.

Think of the joy! Play in the freedom! You're a child of the Father of the universe and have been given the thrilling potential for endless panoramas of self-discovery, friendship and relationship, and untold spiritual expansion.

We, unlike our animal neighbors, *know that we know*, and have the power to make decisions. Your will is the unstoppable transforming force that can bring you to endless vistas of adventure and courage, filled with complete joy, hard work, and love; that is, if you PRAY.

> That which the enlightened and reflective human imagination of spiritual teaching and leading wholeheartedly and unselfishly wants to do and be, becomes measurably creative in accordance with the degree of mortal dedication to the divine doing of the Father's will. When man goes in partnership with God, great things may, and do happen.
>
> —*The Urantia Book*

Your will is yours to control and expand and it supplies positive and negative experiences; it's the door to spiritual progress or material regression. No other influence—even God—can change a course you forcefully and consistently choose, or halt its inevitable results.

Wholeheartedness determines what we'll experience and achieve and how we'll change. Halfhearted decisions and actions do nothing but bring frustration and dissatisfaction (actually, the gifts from God to get us off our butts). Half-heartedness is "having one foot on the platform and the other on the train" or trying to swim without stepping into the pool. Wholeheartedness is the key to movement.

Your will can bring the joy of friendship and service, hours of laughter and good times, or it can bring the dead isolation of an empty home and meaningless material objects. Your focus can bring the pull, flight, and journey of achievement, new learning, and adaptation, or the encasing and obscuring layers of inaction, fear, and self-pity. Your direction can improve the world by doing the "impossible" and showing a spiritual vision, or cause self-decay with cynical anxiety and whining criticism about your circumstances.

We're always at the pivot and crux of all universe possibility and attainment and should be overjoyed and eternally motivated by the prospect of surpassing our greatest achievements as they become yesterday's preschool towards God's university. Problems, goals, desires, and urges are the proponents of prayer who say "Think about your problems. Sing to God. Find out what he wants you to do. Go out and do it, because you're a direct child of your universe Parent!"

Now that we have a good understanding of the power of attitude, let's look at prayer and see the ramifications of various attitudes. It's our goal to meet life's challenge, minus the interference of restrictive attitudes, by discovering and gently replacing them with lighthearted and jubilant strength and willingness. When we stop to pray, free from these mind blocks, our souls are released to speak the desires of time and the longings of eternity.

They're ready to be supercharged.

The Consequences of Your Attitudes

Your attitudes have a direct effect on if and how you pray. So, if you want to have effective prayers, you need to reflect on your attitudes and continually improve them, especially the negative ones. Negative attitudes restrict your mind and virtually block all communication from God. Negative attitudes keep you a prisoner.

Prejudice is the most caustic and restrictive influence, and naturally, the worst attitude to have toward or in prayer. Prejudice is prejudging, assuming, predicting, closing the mind. When we're prejudiced, we often believe we know what's coming and what should be delivered, impatiently demanding a result, or requiring a definite course of action from God. And guess what? We're left frustrated, confused, and angry with God because he wasn't the spiritual pizza driver we wanted.

Prejudice in approaching prayer is just as disastrous and dark as prejudice to our brothers and sisters because, in each case, the truth and joy of interaction with another is blocked by slabs of misunderstanding, fear, and anxiety, or willful hate. Prejudice is a barrier to the real God.

You see, the usual source of our prejudice—when not born of intentional hatred—is the need to survive real dangers and compelling need. Our animal heritage focuses on how to survive as an animal: Avoid all threats and get basic needs met while hoarding energy. Your basic survival instincts say: "Minimize risk by trying to predict the outcome before you begin, and conserve as much energy as you can since you don't know when you'll get more food. Reduce wear and tear on the body and avoid death."

So, we often feel compelled to avoid change because it takes energy and strength and may put us in scary situations. If we do this, fear promises that we'll never be taken off guard and will have the energy to go on. *This is the illusion of control* that's helped humanity survive, but it's also frozen many in the ice of conforming dead belief and habit.

> The divinity that shapes our ends is in ourselves . . . All that a man achieves or fails to achieve is the direct result of his own thoughts.
>
> —James Lane Allen

In the face of an uncertain future, we often resort to expectations and predictions that limit and blind us to wonderful possibilities, just so we don't have to feel afraid of the unknown.

Let's say I have a very large sack of seeds and a very large plot of land. I think, "I want to grow some great vegetables. I know the best way." So, I go and plant in a small corner that I just know will produce the most: Why should I waste time in the other sections? Time moves on and I end up with nothing because I concentrated too much on the small area I've selected, drowned the plants, and overlooked its poor soil. I have nothing because I thought I knew the way it was supposed to happen. I was prejudiced; I prejudged the possibilities and the outcome.

In the end, if our prejudice isn't born of intentional destructiveness, God will lead us to real liberating spiritual vision in daily tasks, prayer, and inner-worship—communion. He gives us a new section of land, a new bag of seeds, and all we need to nourish the garden of our souls. God knows your challenges and *real* intentions. He's cheering for you every step of the way, through every challenge and decision in your life.

If we're honestly and absolutely willing to see and absorb truth, this spiritual vision becomes the endless display of divine reality that leads to solid personal achievement. But, if we approach prayer with set notions, we soon deceive ourselves with fantasies of God's guidance that are really just imaginary expressions of what *we want to hear.* Our lives tumble down a slope of pointless pursuits, our minds and hearts overwhelmed by unfulfilled spiritual longing.

Sometimes it's not until we try everything else, even fantasies of God's guidance, that the way in our minds is cleared for real spiritual impact and travel. Prayer is the ticket.

The answer is to constantly foster and go with a spiritual attitude. Start out pure as a child to release your original state of sincerity, a hunger for the truth, and the faith to accept the delicious experiences God brings. Be dedicated to God's will through love and service to others. Get reenergized every day through prayer and inner-worship.

If you pour your heart out to God and touch the spiritual guiding stars, you'll soon feel the loving embrace of the Creator and surmount all attitude problems. Your life will be a celebration of relationship to God and your universe family and an expression of His will. You'll begin to have more and more moments of delight where you forget time and taste eternity.

The Function of Prayer

Our basic material needs drive us and spiritual needs *lead* us to the same place—the sanctuary of prayer. We all face challenges and the pull to achieve and frequently crave to thank a perfect someone and ask Him for help in this experience. Needs, desires, and urges are the sparks that bring willing and open people to the Creator through the steps of belief in Him, The Universal Spiritual Way, dedication to His will, and vigorous application of prayer and other spiritual techniques.

There are two categories of need: material and spiritual. Before spiritual needs can be satisfied, the material must be met. As many religious workers in poor countries attest, it's extremely difficult to teach spiritual truth to someone when they haven't eaten for a couple days, are dying of disease, or have no safe place to live. God certainly gets through in all situations to all people, but spiritual growth is slowed down when the person is incessantly struggling to make it, even to stay alive, using all their time to find necessities.

When the material foundation exists, it's easier to spend time thinking about spiritual truth and enjoying spiritually-nourishing practices. You've been given time to think and begin quality prayer and worship.

> Self-actualizing individuals (more matured, more fully human), by definition, already suitably gratified in their basic needs, are now motivated in other higher ways . . .
>
> —Abraham Maslow,
> *The Farther Reaches of Human Nature*

With the basic human needs fulfilled, the signals of the Spirit shine brighter. Our minds and hearts are flooded with divine brilliance and the growth-challenge from God becomes clear. If we embrace this experience, we soon discover a new and utterly unexpected need: We have to thank God.

With total gratitude and celebration, we spontaneously pour our love and devotion into the divine channel as children running in a stream. Prayer leads to the ultimate spiritual experiences: worship and communion to divine immersion. But, before we can realize the full potential of prayer, we've got to fill basic material needs and fully understand and address our spiritual ones.

If you're determined to have effective, profound prayer, you've got to be willing to make it a high priority and gather the resources necessary. Attempting ideal prayer without supporting it is like trying to climb a mountain without shoes or food. If we're serious, it's time to get down to business and deliver what's needed to allow the process to bear and continue bearing spiritual fruits.

Understanding and filling celestial want becomes our priority and begins with the urge for growth and truth to accelerate it. We begin with knowledge of our spiritual status—our spiritual poverty—and are soon enticed into the quickening thrill of the universe perfection adventure.

You and I have a flame drawing us to God and constantly suggesting worlds of undreamed-of personal achievement. These revelations gradually replace our current ideals with emerging divine visions, infusing all actions and thought. The mountaintops of our highest achievements soon become the plains leading to new and more fantastic peaks.

The center of growth is your soul. As you begin to nourish your soul by praying and worshipping, huge desires for growth flood your heart. You begin to cultivate this experience by increased praying and are eventually able to feel your soul during more times in the day: driving and commuting, shopping, on the job, in the classroom, in nature, working on the car, changing the diapers, giving a lecture, scrubbing floors, etc. Your life becomes enriched (all work becomes sacred) because you've wholeheartedly prayed and dedicated yourself to soul growth.

And while our minds are indispensable for reaching goals and dealing with problems, prayer's goal is to make us less thinking and more insightful, more realizing. During inner-worship, we eventually suspend thought and express our hearts to God to find release from all human limitations and discover renewed power for good deeds. Since the mind relies on basic assumptions as starting points, the suspension of thinking allows God to place new gems of insight. This brings new assumptions and translates logic to higher levels for fresh conclusions and personal success.

Prejudice and old assumptions can be transformed in the light of living truth. Prayer and worship brings us basic building blocks or starting points—givens. There's no way to prove the existence of your soul or God, yet these become the foundation for subsequent thinking: If we're certain and divinely assured that they're true, we're free to visualize and think new ideas and explanations that transcend the results of material-minded thinking.

Without the assumption of vast geologic time, the theory of evolution could not stand. Minus the liberation of realizing your relation to God, you crumple and crack. By accepting the new revelations of God, you allow your foundation to be transformed and expanded.

"God, touch me! God, hold me! Show me!" Our desire for divine contact becomes total and encompasses all waking moments. The ecstasy and assurance of universe destiny unfolds to the burgeoning soul to caress the yearning heart.

This continual communion begins to emerge as we practice the enriching habit of telling God everything that's in our hearts and minds and bringing Him into all decisions and activities.

This doesn't mean that we have it easy, but that we're given more strength and presence to concentrate and cheerfully participate in all circumstances. Our souls are supercharged.

Prayer is great, and exclusive prayer sessions are superb remedies for human limitations: Everyone from children overdosing on pop-culture, farmers worrying about weather and government, to insurance professionals and circus performers, needs prayer to detach from life and the unending stream of thoughts. When you're alone and open to prayer, the hour's fluttering concerns become distant and still as you walk to the divine spot, your place of peace and communion with God.

Here you surrender your will to God to learn His will. Instead of having your willpower weakened, you load up profound energy and power to aid the divine project and your progressive goals. You step with prayer to the realm of worship and communion; you intensely adore and listen to God.

Although some see accepting God's will as servitude and degradation to a divine taskmaster (usually based on anthropomorphized God ideas), a follower of The Universal Spiritual Way feels exuberance and liberation. She becomes more spiritual and has access to boundless strength, becoming independent of fear and anxiety: This is LIBERATION—total salvation—and only occurs through prayer-release. Overcoming human limitations is the most pressing of all needs.

> You can never go beyond My Love and Care. Remember that. No evil can befall you. Circumstances I bless and use must be the right ones for you.
>
> But I know always that the first step is to lay your will before Me as an offering, ready that I shall do what is best, sure that, if you trust Me, what I do for you will be best.
>
> Your second step is to be sure, and to tell me so, that I am Powerful enough to do everything . . . that no miracle is impossible with me . . .
>
> Then leave all with Me. Glad to leave all your affairs in a Master Hand. Sure of safety and protection. Remember you cannot see the future. I can.
> You could not bear it. So only little by little can I reveal it to you. Accept My Will and it will bring you joy.
>
> —*God Calling*, A.J. Russell, editor

When you base your life on this perfect prayer technique, this sublime conversation, you begin to create a world based on The Universal Spiritual Way. You're gradually drawn to others who share your beliefs and motivations to project a common vision of a better group, community, nation, and planet. This unification is only possible because it's based on a common vision given by the Creator: God reveals His will for the group to all who are willing to see it and work toward it. Society is slowly, very slowly, coalescing under the vision of God's will. We're doing it with prayer and service.

Sincere heart-expression through the soul conserves and synthesizes values for the individual and group. God brings far-reaching constellations of people together to unite to achieve His vision. We're mostly unconscious of how we're guided together, but inevitably, when we pray for help on a good project aligned with God's plan, we suddenly have the right people and resources at just the right time.

Prayer unerringly brings societal unity for action and the inevitable changes from such service. Eventually, prayer will lead humankind to a future so far beyond our imagination that we'd swear it's the heaven of our dreams. Prayer begins as a personal expression, expands to form group expression and activity, and becomes the technique for unifying and uplifting civilization, which in turn helps the individual.

Prayer is the only way to begin and sustain the journey. Prayer is the breath of your soul.

Spiritual Truths

We need prayer to know God and grow.

Our attitudes determine what we'll experience and do.

Prayer is the act of talking to God for help or thankfulness.

Sincerity, a longing for truth, and faith are the foundation for salvation.

Inner-worship of God is the gateway to all spiritual power—supercharging.

Wholeheartedness is the basis for change.

And this I do believe above all, especially in times of greater discouragement, that I must BELIEVE—that I must believe in my fellow men—that I must believe in myself—that I must believe in God—if life is to have any meaning.

—Margaret Chase Smith, *This I Believe*

Nourishment for Your Soul

Getting Power for Your Journey

Chapter 2

The intellectual growth of a child is a miracle of evolution. Just think, each of us, initially, couldn't understand what we were seeing, hearing, and thinking. We could express hunger, pain, and a few basic emotions but could barely control our bodies. We were absolutely and utterly dependent on our parents and caregivers.

But soon we learned words to match things in our world and express more of our expanding desires. The power of language and the knowledge we gained brought us new outer experiences, self-knowledge, and competencies. Our understanding of the world and ourselves led us to a life of discovery and possibility, pain and joy, failure and success, and growth.

Knowledge is the beginning of progress. And spiritual knowledge can be the beginning of eternal life—starting *now.*

We've briefly discussed the soul so far, but to pray with real power we need a fuller understanding. Even though our beliefs and understandings don't determine whether we'll be resurrected, they do control our *rate of progress* and the quantity of spiritual fruits we'll experience now. They define how we experience our salvation. They decide the breadth and impact of our spiritual liberation. By having a clear understanding of the soul, we have a river, rather than a straw, to deliver the life-giving water. Knowledge is power.

The Nature of the Soul

You're engaged in the adventure of the ages: God gives you life and the ability to choose and a companion (the Spirit within) who makes eternal progression possible. The Spirit of God is the medium by which you experience and talk to God, as well as the way you receive infinite treasures, the most important being your soul. This Spirit is an *actual* piece of God that works for Him in your mind to help you transcend limited thinking and achieve spiritual thought.

When you decide to follow the will of God the Father, truly bringing God into your decisions and following His leading, you allow your spirit companion to create a new, more real part of yourself. You cooperate with the spirit to build this new inner place for your self-consciousness, in addition to the places of mind and body. It's a new home with interesting rooms, new appliances, larger windows, and better surroundings. The best way to create this house is by wholeheartedly trying to pray, worship, and do the Father's will.

Your soul is more real than your mind or body. When you strive to grow, you feel it more each day. Your soul is the part of you that yearns for and recognizes truth. Your soul is the *real you* that you're becoming. Like a spiritual car that will take you to the next world, your soul is a spiritual treasure house of all the good that you've selflessly done.

When I talk about houses of mind, body, and soul, I refer to elements of you. Please understand that you're not your mind, body, or soul, but the person in them, the one (the personality) who knows that you're awake and can make decisions. Your personality can touch experiences in thought, physical sensation, and spiritual reality. Your personality (you) is your identity. You (a unique person) sit in the middle of a life wardrobe, surrounded by God's garments, and can combine and use them as needed: alone, two at a time, or all together. You're not the clothing, but *the one inside*.

As you affect mind, body, and soul, you're exercising your identity *inside* them, with your inner spirit as your companion. While it's obvious these aspects of self are necessary to get around, the proper hierarchy shows that Spirit leads soul and mind; soul enables mind; and mind leads body. At the core of all elements of self is your decision-making center, your personality.

We should identify with (touch and imitate) the Father's Spirit through the soul by intense prayer and worship. We should then act to alter ourselves and the tools of soul, mind, and body to approach and attain spiritual standards.

The sweet prize of spiritualization is the soul. It's the soul that loyally channels all spirit fruits: the salvation from all limitations and the gateway to eternal life. The soul allows us to display amazing courage, persistent effort, soothing kindness and understanding, happiness, character growth, and all that's admirable through all events. When we act from the soul we have access to an endless array of spiritual expressions and instruments that dramatically enhance our ability to both do the Father's will and surpass our initial standards.

But, we must keep it fed, energized by God.

> However far back we go in the history of the race, we can never find a time or place where man was not conscious of the soul and of a divine power on which his life depended.
>
> —Christopher Dawson

Our minds will always be surprised and delighted by transformations brought by the Spirit through the soul. The most important of these fruits—the growth of your soul—is the vehicle, the house, the dwelling, the cradle which takes you to the afterlife.

Your soul creates desires not found in mind or body. The more you feel the soul through prayer and worship, the more you yearn to stay, the more you celebrate your experience of God-consciousness.

Your soul has its own cravings and expressions, preludes to your eternal future of incredible manifestations of sincerity, truth-hunger, and faith-power-acceptance. When you embrace your soul, you embody these qualities of personality and relish opportunities for courage and hard work.

But, when you make the effort to grow, you need more spiritual food. When you follow God's lead—when you exercise—you use real spiritual energy that must be replenished if you're to stay on the path and do great things, and if you want to be happy.

Prayer and inner-worship provide sustenance for the soul: We soon realize it's our greatest need. The soul must repeatedly receive nourishment from contact with the Creator in sincere, intense, profound prayer and inner-worship of God. It must grow from the exercise of grappling with problems, attaining goals, and coordinating these acts with the Father's will. Neglect of either nourishment or exercise has terrible effects, far worse than can be inflicted on the body.

Prayer is the very breath of your soul. Just think of a time when you held your breath as long as you could. How did that feel to be desperate for air? We can't ignore our most important physical needs and should develop the same acute sensitivity to our souls. They need nourishment from the spiritual atmosphere *just as much.* Prayer provides this channel to spiritual energy and is an expression of the soul and the doorway to inner-worship—active, perfect contact with God.

In the song of prayer and inner-worship, the soul is nourished and contacts our heart, improves our attitude, and stimulates us to action. The ideal place to work from is the soul, and the ideal way to care for that home is through prayer. The key is to believe and act on the truths of The Universal Spiritual Way.

God and His Role

As I look at the Creator's design and Universe, I'm awed by the unity and grandeur of the world and the aspects that make up myself. The Creator provides the unification of these parts and a universal spiritual technique: If you desire good health, clear thinking, principled success in relationship or business or any worthy area, then take the spiritual attitude and come sincerely, with a desire for truth and the faith to attain your vision. Act bravely and vigorously.

If we want to find true happiness, if we want true progress, if we want real peace, assurance, and eternal security, we must accept God's revelations and work hard to follow His guidance. And, prayer is the most effective technique to maintain this cycle of growth. *Just hoping for and visualizing something doesn't make it come true.*

Conversation with God is the essence of prayer. *But* we must come with enthusiasm and faith to accept the personal beauties only found and received by interacting with that other person—God. And, it's our conception of God that's a gateway or a wall.

If you're God trying to reach me, you have little chance to get through or help me grow if I won't accept your reality, don't believe you're there, or have preconceptions of who you are.

To begin to know and understand God's personality, we've got to realize that our conceptions of Him are incomplete, finite, imperfect, and in need of eternal improvement. Picture the ideal person: the most intelligent, loving, well-balanced, strong, kind, and powerful being who rules and created all, and I promise it's just the beginning of endless visions of God's greatness.

> I will bless the Lord at all times;
> His praise shall continually be in my mouth.
> My soul makes its boast in the Lord;
> let the afflicted hear and be glad.
> O magnify the Lord with me,
> and let us exalt his name together!
> I sought the Lord, and he answered me,
> and delivered me from all my fears.
> Look to him, and be radiant;
> so your faces shall never be ashamed . . .
>
> —Psalm 34:1-5, *The Bible*

God will always transcend our fondest and dearest ideals, softly tugging, beckoning to sublime experiences of truth, beauty, and goodness, and moments of communion and worship.

The Source of all is neither male nor female, but I encourage you to think of God as your perfect loving Universal Father who wants the best for everyone and gives unconditional goodness and love when we need it, in the way we need it, for as long as we need it.

God manifests as God the Father and God the Son and God the Spirit, but it's God the Father who gave each of us a unique piece of Himself and who's direction we should follow. Doing the will of the Father is the key to eternity. The Father leads, challenges, and involves all of us, while God the Son nurtures, comforts, and heals us. He draws us to other spiritually-minded people and heavenward in projects to support the divine plan.

At the most primary level, God manifests as God the Father, God the Mother-Son, and God the Spirit: the Father, Son, and Spirit. And it is God the Spirit that is the expression of the relationship between God the Father and God the Mother-Son. The first person of the trinity loves *as* a father, not like a father. Fatherly love isn't male or female: It's divine, perfect, infinite, and eternal.

Our names for God may vary and really don't matter that much. But, if you're open, you'll experience the first person of deity *as a father, not a male.*

The Creator is not an illusion of the mystical imagination, but a real person—the source of all persons. He passionately enjoys intimate conversation with His children and is thrilled when they manifest His will and realize their best, ideal happiness.

Our Maker's will is absolute and encompasses the eternal past, present, and future with an incredibly well-coordinated plan. God's will is expressed in this plan which includes everything and everyone in joyful celebration of life and the realization of all spiritual potential: simple matter, elements, plants, microbes, insects, animals, the planetary organism, the universe, and each of us. Everything has an interdependent role that brings personal achievement and progressive evolution.

In this stupendous universe-wide enterprise, please know that God's will is the revelation of love that shows how we should achieve the beautiful, the good, and the true, while having success in all noble aspects of life.

Just think of the significance of your unique part of the plan in every experience of your life, whether on the train, in the cubical, in the stockyard, in the nursery, on vacation, at a party, in the store, and in all places. If you choose the Father's will through prayer and worship, if you ask to know, and work hard, every good ambition or desire will be fulfilled—on Earth or in the afterlife.

You'll eventually have your deepest longings of every kind fulfilled in eternity, that is, if they're positive and in alignment with the will of the Creator, and if you *persistently* work hard toward that vision.

God's plan might seem like a straightjacket to some, but, what God wants us to do and the way he wants us to live is exactly what we'd choose if we knew all He did. God's future plan for you is beyond the best you've experienced but will only be realized if you're not allowed to know it: You must be required to make decisions based on faith and inner guidance.

Since we hardly ever have access to God's future knowledge, we must accept by *faith* that His love always brings us the best path and the best technique.

This is part of what defines us as humans, as the faith-children of God. What a privilege! What a great and awesome world of promise and adventure, the sublime heritage of the ages!

You'll rarely know the future, but you can transcend time to find a life of spectacular spiritual achievement and unexpected glory. The Creator satisfies our greatest and deepest longings not by spoiling the story by blurting out its ending, but by allowing us to co-create an eternal career of divine cooperation.

Is it a surprise that God hears our prayers? Every utterance or thought that's born of sincerity instantly flashes to God, traveling over space and time to bring back instant contact through His Spirit. The Spirit within you provides the direct link. And, if you keep your ideal of God in mind, you realize that God is always listening and craves contact with all His children across a vast creation.

Don't we feel that natural desire for contact with loved ones? Haven't we delighted at the arrival of an old friend? Isn't the purpose of life to have relationships?

Since we (as imperfect and confused as we are) are able to show great love and experience real longing, we should accept that God does as well. He has a love and desire for contact born from endless yesterdays, reaching through countless tomorrows. God wants to talk to us and hear our expressions. But, while he knows all we do and think, he can't deliver His message unless we completely open the door with *firm, sustained* intention.

Prayer and God

Our motivation and attitude toward God and the universe ensures or blocks reception of His presence. When we express the sincere longing of our heart and ask for His will, there's an immediate divine entrance into our soul. It's like gentle steady rain, beautiful sunlight, or a soft breeze. It's LOVE. When we use our sincerity and hunger for what's right, we can be certain that we'll offer prayers that concern our deepest needs and prepare us for the perfect answers.

When praying, remember that God knows your needs (from the beginning of creation) before you do and constantly tries to meet them. Of course, God can't meet our needs if we block His attempts with pride or fear, or stop the delivery of these blessings by limiting our actions.

We must give all and believe we're spiritually cared for.

All your real needs can be met! These necessities are intended to provide that wonderful impetus to move forward in spirituality toward endless satisfaction and broad landscapes of possibility. If we trust God, we're assured that all good is eventually realized at the perfect moment when we can recognize and benefit from these splendors.

When we talk to God, we should come with total confidence that praying is going to bring the best solution for our problems and is the prelude to adoration for God. Nothing can stop our ideal prayers. Prayer is a flame that dissolves our frigid fear, inflexibility, and confusion. Our loving Parent is infinitely and eternally determined to have contact with us across all places and times and will always bring us just what we need if we'll accept it. Let's not forget.

This conversation with God must be built on a matrix of dynamic belief in God as a perfect loving parent. To reach real prayer, we must believe The Universal Spiritual Way which will inform and instruct our decisions and give reliable, lasting access to God. Without belief in God, prayer isn't possible and sinks to the level of psychological hope and desired magic.

Prayer causes us to visualize a perfect God and continually improves this vision by direct contact with Him. But, when we have the sincerity to accept the inner experience, we find it's the greatest one in life—God. The only way to achieve an approach to the Divine by prayer is to accept the truths of The Universal Spiritual Way: The most important one is that you are a child of God.

But, belief isn't all! Since we want prayer to bring full blessings, whether they be growth opportunities, personal improvement, or needs met, we must be completely unified in sincere devotion to God's will. Please realize that God's will brings the best for the largest number of us, for the longest time, individually and collectively. You get your needs met as the group gets its needs met; as you grow, the group benefits. Each result helps the other.

If our prayers align with the Creator's plan, they're fully answered. If we pray with utmost sincerity, *even if we're misguided*, God still has an opportunity to bring real truth and strength to enable us to seek what's really good for us. Remember: Any prayer that's not in agreement with the direct will of God or not in accord with that will, has no chance of being fulfilled. Real prayer always eventually reaches its goal and delivers us to the world of inner-worship of God.

Worship, in its truest sense, comes after and is improved by prayer. Worship is the deepest contact we have with God and is the act of thanking, adoring, honoring, and listening to Him with absolute saturation and concentration in total self-forgetfulness. Worship is our greatest experience and integrates with the soul, mind, and body. It is "the pearl of great price" that doesn't involve asking or expecting anything: The moment you request something, you're not in worship, but have gone back to prayer.

If you want to supercharge your soul, don't make that the goal of your worship of God. Just adore. Just thank. Just listen. Just embrace. Just accept whatever God reveals.

Since this book doesn't have room for an adequate discussion of inner-worship, let's simply remember that it transcends all experience and should be the worthy daily goal of all sincere people who pray. Worship is to life what color is to a rainbow: new realms and dimensions, the full transformational communion with God, immersion in the Divine.

Inner-worship of God supercharges your soul.

I've put a lot of stress on belief as a key enabler of your journey. I know this is counter to much of what we're told about spiritual progress and real happiness and can bring up images of intolerance and persecution. Yet, belief—after sincerity, desire for truth, and faith—is the *most important factor* in religious and spiritual achievement.

Our thoughts lead us to God, not our feelings. The mind is a gift from God that enables us to experience the world around and inside us.

Belief—acceptance of inner divine experiences, spiritual realities—opens the mind door through which an experience of

God and spiritual treasures flow; it mobilizes your energizes and helps you to adopt effective techniques for growth. Belief doesn't open God's heart, but instead, frees our hearts to live again, to grow. With wholehearted acceptance of inner experience, a natural belief in God emerges.

If we have the sincerity and desire to change our current incompatible beliefs (God can't be a person; God can't be trusted; etc.), we discover and accept the truths of The Universal Spiritual Way and use these to leap into unending revelations and personal progress.

So, let's review: Full spiritual growth and the resulting God-relationship is impossible without belief in the Creator. All sincere people who respond to the Spirit within will be resurrected after death. Those who don't accept spiritual reality and its growth principles can hardly enjoy in this earth life the assurance and benefits of actively cooperating with God in a supportive relationship.

Spirituality and growth is rooted in an active relationship with the Creator and is limited if we stubbornly deny His existence. To grow, we must patiently do God's will. To fully follow and understand God's leading, we must have a conscious relationship with Him. To have a conscious relationship with Him, we must accept that He exists. We must believe. We must accept the spiritual experience within we've already been given. The beginning of spiritual growth isn't membership in a church or affiliation with an organization (although everyone should seek a good spiritual community) but, instead, total acceptance of God by believing in Him.

The mind is God's gift, crucial to life, but we don't realize this until we accept that very Creator. We need to let our hearts touch God and express themselves through our minds. We should believe with faith!

Prayer and the Mind

Prayer is the expression of the attitude of the soul toward the Father's spirit within you. When you enter genuine prayer, you're responding to the urge to pray from your soul: You use your mind to communicate the attitude of your soul to its Creator. Using our minds to know the Father and follow His leading is the key to progress. Your future is determined by the way you think, which determines the way you'll act.

The mind is the bridge between the material and spiritual. It makes sense of what it experiences inside and outside of the body. Our minds create thoughts/pictures to represent the experience of God, as well as everything we experience of the outer world. The quality and direction of your thoughts is the raw material for your decisions, which will lead to actions that increase or decrease your spiritual experience and the growth of your soul.

Be sure to let your spiritual thoughts rejuvenate and transform your mind so you can transform your life. Your thoughts, not your feelings, are the key to spiritual progress. It can be your privilege to spread the transforming power of the spirit to the outer world through the channel of your mind. It can be joyful to have your mind illuminated with the infinite beauty and love of the Father.

And, the most effective way to open your mind to such a continual rebirth is to pray for it to be transformed. You should use your thoughts and actions to express the attitudes and desires of your soul—*the real you.* With such a combination of improved thinking and action aligned with God's will, your soul will grow and your life will change.

The mind makes thoughts we can move around, like Lego® blocks. With our cooperation, it does its best to make pictures of what should be (God's will) to inspire and lead us to change the outer world of family, friends, co-workers, etc. Mind prepares the way for prayer, sees its revelations, and makes plans afterward. Please remember: The garden of your soul is best nourished with beautiful, unified noble thoughts of faith.

It's up to you. You determine what thoughts you have and which ones you amplify. Be careful what you spread on the garden of your mind. Keep it as free as you can of negativity, fear, anger, and other toxic emotions and animal desires and attitudes. Remove the clutter and debris so the light of the spirit can shine through.

Mind is incredibly important. It has an interesting beginning: In the morning of childhood, we get a strong urge to socialize and begin to form thoughts. At the start, we're mostly self-centered, but we do crave relationship with others and even practice this in our minds.

We start to hold conversations in our minds and find it necessary to create imaginary friends and characters who are always accessible. These imaginary people become the basis for future interactions and thoughts, as we play with them, talk about life, and ask them for help. In fact, most of us still think in conversation, usually hearing another voice.

The voice we usually hear and respond to is our alter ego. The most important implication for prayer is that, before we even try to talk to God, we've practiced reaching out, asking for inner help anywhere and anytime, when no human is around. Once we begin to recognize God, the inner conversation can become truly profound as it shifts from our imaginary friend to our Divine Parent—our best and most-real friend.

Prayer is a divine conversation based on the childhood inner dialogue. But, while inner conversation starts as a fantasy need, it really is the pattern for real contact with God through prayer. God continually improves our ideal of Him to gradually and endlessly bring more expanded and real experiences. Enlightened understanding of God-the-person is the gateway for all future spiritual experiences.

Genuine contact with the Creator occurs when we come as children with open hearts, allowing God to replace our thoughts with the visions of eternity and the joys of His presence. If we maintain an attitude of faith and consecration, our unconscious fantasy is replaced by solid, indisputable divine contact. But, we must make continual, repeated wholehearted efforts.

Most prayers (certainly the best prayers) should show that we're doing something to solve our problems: They should ideally lead us to be totally motivated. But, we've got to remember that we're the imperfect trying to communicate and reach the Perfect. Inevitably, it's going to be hard and bring disappointment and unexpected results, such as between infant and parent.

> Prayer is the breath of the soul and should lead you to be persistent in your attempt to ascertain the Father's will. If any one of you has a neighbor, and you go to him at midnight and say: "Friend, lend me three loaves, for a friend of mine on a journey has come to see me, and I have nothing to set before him"; and if your neighbor answers, "Trouble me not, for the door is now shut and the children and I are in bed; therefore I cannot rise and give you bread," you will persist, explaining that your friend hungers, and that you have no food to offer him. I say to you, though your

> neighbor will not rise and give you bread because he is your friend, yet because of your importunity he will get up and give you as many loaves as you need. If, then, persistence will win favors even from mortal man, how much more will your persistence in the spirit win the bread of life for you from the willing hands of the Father in heaven. Again I say to you: Ask and it shall be given you; seek and you shall find; knock and it shall be opened to you. For every one who asks receives; he who seeks finds; and to him who knocks the door of salvation will be opened.
>
> —Jesus from *The Urantia Book*

When we come to God with sincere wholeheartedness, His spiritual gifts can flow to us. He answers our material prayers with spiritual power and quality, not a cornucopia of material presents. Our prayers can be egoistic or altruistic; we can be materialistic or spiritual. Ask yourself, "How often do I pray? For whom? For what?"

We need to realize that despite our finite imperfection and confusion, missed opportunities and mistakes, even our willing stubbornness or real cruelty, the Father's love is unconditional and unfailing. If we remember to keep our attitudes true and develop habits of hard work and bravery, nothing can stop us on our way to Paradise—the destination of eternal life. Our sincere prayers become the fuel and nourishment for the outstretched journey to forever vistas.

Prayer actually increases our spiritual capacity and is the first step in becoming more than we are. Ideal prayer leads us to inner-worship of God. Prayer can really lead us to supercharge our souls in the total immersion of God.

By total belief in our place as beloved children of the Father and embracing the truths of The Universal Spiritual Way, we make it possible for our souls to talk to God. By profoundly praying each day, by trying just a little more each day, we make it possible for the spirit within to make us more than we are. We begin doing the impossible. We are the faith-children of God on an incredible, endless universe adventure.

We sing to our Creator with the rushing breath of our souls.

Spiritual Truths

We need prayer to know God and grow.

Our attitudes determine what we'll experience and do.

Prayer is the act of talking to God for
help or thankfulness.

Our souls are only satisfied and nourished by
prayer and the inner-worship of God.

There is no growth without prayer.

True prayer is to our personal God.

Sincerity, a longing for truth, and faith are
the foundation for salvation.

Courage and hard work are the dynamos of growth.

Wholeheartedness is the basis for change.

What, then, is the greatest power in the universe? I believe that it is the mechanism by which man on earth establishes a connection that provides the flow of power between the mighty Creator and himself, between the great God who scattered the stars in the infinite night sky and the creature made in His own image: man. The flow of power between the Creator and man is the world's greatest power . . . And it is released and transmitted by means of a mechanism known as prayer.

—Norman Vincent Peale,
Power of the Plus Factor Factor

The Incredible Power of Prayer

Finding Total Hope and Transformation

Chapter 3

A while ago, I lived in the mountains of Colorado and decided to go for a little drive. As I rumbled along a dusty dirt road, I came across a familiar old mine site—a crumbling stone building surrounded by snow, under a dark sky. There was a bolted, locked door, old, rusting iron train tracks, and heaps of rusted gears, a rotting steam boiler, and twisted pipe. The people who worked this mine had very high hopes, but it was clear that the mining operation hadn't been the success they hoped for.

How many lives mirror that scene? How many people lay weak and pointless tracks to illusive or destructive places? But, as bad as it can get, there's always an inner divine solution to lead them down the road to progress and happiness.

Prayer and inner-worship is like carbon in pig iron: By simply adding 1.7 percent carbon you produce elastic, strong, enduring steel to build bridges, city towers, schools, and other structures. If we took at least twenty-four minutes a day for inner spiritual nourishment, what would happen? If we disciplined our fragmented selves, where would the Maker lead us? What would we find and become? We'd see that the miracles of nature, science, and fiction are eclipsed by real spiritual progress. The Creator brings mysterious changes to the 100 percent willing human . . . once limited, fearful, doomed to death, now a liberated eternal universe citizen.

Our Challenge

We're born in a sea of need; we must cope with life's internal and external challenges. We must choose a reaction in our minds to progress or regress, reach life or sink into patterns of passivity and death. This fire of need challenges us to expand past the twilight of infancy, through the experimentation of childhood, past self-discovering adolescence, into adulthood, and eventually divine realization.

Need is that grand and all-pervading stimulus that can cause us to graduate from physical requirements and psychological yearnings to faith-acceptance and spiritual achievement—contact with the Creator and service to others.

These life requirements inevitably lead to us to form goals and, the plans to achieve them. For instance, let's say I'm a young man and have just moved away from my parents, friends, and hometown. All my needs used to be met in a comfortable place. But, after the initial excitement of traveling cross-country and finding a home, a pain and yearning develops: I need to socialize and make new friends.

This socialization need helps me realize that my goal is to have human contact that will lead to friendships and relationships, new circles of support and mutual affection. My plan is to use all opportunities to be friendly and join the local tennis club. By carrying out my plan, I reach the goal of social interaction and fill the need of friendship and relationship. My family calls and I say, "I'm great!"

But, this scenario isn't the full picture. Growth not only occurs by carrying out a plan, but by adapting and modifying it as we go along. There are thousands of variations to the example of the "new kid in town." Plans and problems were made for each other. I could've discovered that, while the plan made sense, I was unable to find a group that met when I was free from work; I may have seen that the people in the group were much older and had little in common with me. Or, I may have found that even though I began to meet a lot of great people, I didn't have money to go out and socialize, let alone start dating.

We must accept the slow and gradual realization of our goals. Since we've got to work with evolution, we're required to *patiently* get through the walls, the problems—the brakes on goal-achievement. And, the best way to keep focus and gain strength is through asking for God's advice and power and opportunities to serve others. We should pray.

Problems are fascinating, wonderful gifts, not only because they're the context for growth, but also because they can eliminate perceived need (illusions, unreasonable wants) and open the revelation of *real need* (spiritual craving). The greatest blessing from problems is that they drive us to act, to sit up, reevaluate, create a new plan, and dive in.

We're often led to unsuspectingly forget our original wants (we usually think they're needs) and realize fulfillment and actualization in other neglected or newly realized life areas: This process is only possible with the gift of problems and our willingness to try, move, strive, emerge, and fly. Only prayer and inner-worship of God can sustain this flight.

Although we may eventually accept this as a blessed masterful adventure, there's unavoidable pain, fear, anxiety, sorrow, frustration, disappointment, and uncertainty that must be continually traversed and transfigured. These emotions and states of consciousness emerge when we feel need, fail to reach goals, or go through typical events. But, they can become the materials for building bridges to a new life and new opportunities.

God designed these inner experiences to reveal our limitations, to hint at the uncharted universe of growth, achievement, service, self-forgetfulness, and love. After all, our Father plants real needs in us and provides feelings to lead our hearts to Him. He brings us to the door of dedication to His will that brings fulfillment beyond comprehension. God has our best, eternal interests at heart.

There's a unique, amazing destiny just for you, and prayer is the doorway.

There's no growth without human limitations. After all, since the essence and bliss of life is growth and its destiny (eternity), we must have limitations. What would it be like if you had no barriers, if whatever you wanted or needed, you had, if you were made a perfect, well-balanced, and an ideal reflection of God from the start?

Our barriers should be honored as the stimuli for unlimited growth, endless capacity enlargement, and infinite spiritual experiences. Real happiness, the world beyond our dreams, the most fantastic events and accomplishments, and the most endearing and cherished friendships are only possible by overcoming limitations. *We must grow.* I thank God for limitations and their exclusive gifts! I thank God for prayer!

Our gifts from God are raw, pure potential, and are unfinished. Like unmade boat paddles, these rough forms of body, mind, and soul, have the potential to become superb tools, emancipating us for travel on infinite oceans.

When facing problems and trying to reach goals, we see our limited thoughts and feelings, our fragile and time-bound bodies, our emerging souls, our untested, immature will-power, and even our over-reflective and self-examining tendencies. When we acknowledge these facts, we can experience anguish and anxiety, or we can find celebration and thankfulness: The secret is belief and connection to God.

> Those who invent a religion without God are like those who would gather fruit without trees, have children without parents . . . You cannot pray to a chemical formula, supplicate a mathematical equation, worship a hypothesis, confide in a postulate, commune with a process, serve an abstraction, or hold loving fellowship with a law.
>
> —*The Urantia Book*

The One bringing limitation also supplies transcendence, that is, if we open the door with strong acceptance/belief of the inner experience of God. Our understanding Creator waits to abundantly flood our beings with expansive peace and confident assurance, and relishes the instant that we believe in Him and The Universal Spiritual Way. Here we sit, outlining, dissecting our flaws, restrictions, roadblocks, poor performances, failures, and imperfections, while the majestic Universe Maker longs to weave tenderness and power in our hearts—our consciousness.

Open! Outstretch! Embrace! Accept the fact that you're a child of God and that He'll help you meet all your needs and desires, soothing and immersing you in spiritual confidence and relaxation. Your Divine Parent delivers incomprehensible peace and eternal assurance that everything's going to be fine, that your growth (real bliss and happiness) can't be harmed, and that you'll be given help to meet all your needs and wants.

Even the immensity of inner agony, fear, shame, or confusion never stops God and shouldn't deter us, for it can be a prelude to sublime tranquility and invigoration: You are saved, not by membership, conformity, attire, words, or status, but by belief in divine reality. Yes, if a person is sincerely responding to the spirit within, she will be resurrected, even without belief in The Universal Spiritual Way. *But, why not know full joy now?*

We must pray beyond churches and all groups. We must nurture a personal, direct relationship with God. We must find the truth ourselves, and the truth about ourselves.

When we believe in the truths of The Universal Spiritual Way, peace and assurance form the deep soil for resilient courage and inspiring personal power. Gradually or suddenly, we're filled with these potentials, these watersheds of action. When we choose to accept and act with them—use faith—we go forward as invincible spiritual citizens to transform the earth.

Decision by decision, challenge by challenge, the Father increases our progress and reward, that is, as long as we increase our sincerity, truth-hunger, and faith-action. We must allow His spirit to transform our hearts and minds, our very thoughts. Again, God supplies the tools. We must use them.

When we have moments of total sincerity and faith, predicated on God's will, supported by peace and assurance, we find incredible courage and endless spiritual victory. You achieve what you've never achieved; you do what you thought was impossible, what others said was fantasy. You begin to live your destiny—what you were made for.

A person rooted in fear, anxiety, laziness, and selfishness can hardly value or yield the fruits of a God-nourished person: spiritual courage, divine certainty, and universe action. Yes, we're filled with pressing needs and have many limitations, but we're also remade by the Spirit who provides the power and vision for endless, stunning growth, for a life transcending all limits.

Relationship with God based in prayer and sound inner-worship of God provides total transcendence, liberation, and salvation from all personal limitations: We find courage, confidence, joy, peace, willpower, and enduring growth—*real* happiness.

Supercharged Growth

Prayer is the most effective way to grow. So, if you want to grow, pray. End of story. Prayer spiritualizes and eternalizes our hearts, attitudes, thoughts, and souls, and our growth sends loving service to others, which in turn, can cause them to grow. Our inner endless longing for spiritual accomplishment and deity-embrace is filled to overflowing when our prayers bond us to God.

No limit can be placed on your growth if you give your open heart and actions to God.

Prayer is so powerful that's its effect on personal growth is beyond the full appreciation of our minds and must be comprehended through our souls. Prayer's strength is like rain: It cuts and dissolves rocks, makes soil for growth, nourishes and transmits all life, makes trees soar, carpets the woods, pleases the ear, caresses the hills, enlivens the plains, and delivers all bounty and refreshment, springing to touch the infinite atmosphere.

Consider these effects on the planet and appreciate that prayer causes greater and more unfathomable metamorphoses of our hearts, minds, and souls.

Consider prayer's effect on attitude. As we saw in Chapter 1, attitude is a tendency or disposition toward a person or thing that determines actions and reception of the experience. Attitude is the first circle out from the point of the heart—you, your self-consciousness, your personality.

Envision a human being as a target: In the middle is the point—YOU—the heart that knows it knows, the place of attitude. You use sincerity and choice to create attitude. The second circle is mind, the tool that helps you work and make decisions between the outside world (body, people, places) and the inner one (God, Spirit). Lastly, is the emerging circle of the soul. This is the perceptive tool/lens allowing you clearer spiritual visions and experience, and bringing improved living in all aspects of life.

You can also move from circle to circle. But you must do the work within one circle to enable the next: You must create wholehearted attitudes. Effective prayer, then, is the expression of the spiritual attitudes of faith, truth-hunger, and courage, activated by hard work: It enables us to change ourselves and the world.

So, sitting in the middle of the target, we should realize that we can change it all, even attitude, but only through determination—a wholehearted bull's eye. If you have malice or hatred toward someone, please understand that it encases, rather than frees, and that the remedy is to immerse yourself in God. Ask God to change this tendency and allow full understanding so you may develop an attitude of love and service toward the other person.

Keep reviewing your reactions to people, yourself, and God. If you don't like your attitude, pray for change and allow it to occur through trusting God. Acceptance and trust of God is the most important attitude because it provides the door to discovery and prayer. The heart must believe what it's experiencing by first creating the attitude of a child: sincerity, a desire for truth, and faith-acceptance. These are the original tendencies God provides. It's up to us to cultivate and encourage them in ourselves and others.

When we emerge from this first attitude circle, we can have the full experience of transfiguration. As we sincerely ask for revelation and change, God reveals His will and works with our parts of self, whether they be thoughts, emotions, attitudes, aspirations, ideals, or spiritual visions. With effective prayer and inner-worship, we're able to accelerate endless changes in every part of ourselves, and that delivers endless benefits. REMARKABLE. UNIMAGINABLE. FANTASTIC. MONUMENTAL. GLIMMERING. IDEAL.

Once we fully commit, it's a thrill to follow the inner guidance of the Creator. When we pour our hearts out to God, barriers to growth evaporate. We know that helping our Father achieve His perfect plan will bring the best to everyone and transport us to greatness.

Prayer is the medium, the dialogue of spiritual education. We show up to class by making time for God and seeking His leading. To know and do God's will is the most challenging of tasks and is only accomplished through prayer and inner-worship of God. When we give all to know God's will by prayer and inner-worship, we experience new levels of revelation and inspiration to express that will in every place and every task.

Don't forget that God's will is done through His children and that their daily jobs, as long as they're helpful, are sacred. Only prayer can reveal God's will and bring the sacred dimension to all worthy tasks, illuminating their purpose and energizing our beings, especially our souls.

> The Spirit of God indwelling our souls ever presses us to the fulfillment of His purpose. But we have a certain power of resistance, something as it were of our own—our love—which we can either give or withhold. Election for God and the inner life means the free giving of that active love to Him—siding with Him at all costs. It is so that we become more and more perfect conductors of His holy energy, spreading His love.
>
> —Evelyn Underhill, *The Ways of the Spirit*

The tremendous pull toward other spiritual people of like mind, attitude, and purpose, is due to this spiritualization. Like a magnet on the other side of a wall, when we persistently drill through the blockage, we feel increased attraction to God. This spiritual gravity is the divine compass unerringly leading us to truth, beauty, and goodness, to our loving God, and to others dedicated to His will.

Prayer performs the wonderful service of quenching our deepest needs, the urges transcending mere physical requirements and leading to soul satisfaction. This aspect of ourselves causes yearning for God and Growth. Nothing but prayer and inner-worship will fill the hunger.

Most of us have a lot of distractions: spending too much time at work, getting absorbed in TV, the phone, computers, reading, etc. These take large amounts of time and energy from relaxation, contemplation, prayer, and inner-worship. Sometimes, we attempt to numb or bury spiritual desire with stimulation of body and mind—the surrender to pleasure and inactivity. We can become lazy and apathetic or overactive.

But God is always stirring up the embers of our souls to alert us to the danger of inaction and awaken us to the incredible destiny he has for each of us.

Acceptance of divine destiny and prayerful devotion is the only cure. Through the power of prayer, we're given a new reality that builds higher and higher plateaus of achievement—more elevated experiences that become the bedrock of greater realization.

Our understanding of the world changes as our ideals and concepts are transported to new spiritual levels/contexts that lead to desires for more growth. The desire to grow should encourage prayer, which should bring even more growth urges, action, and the desire for more prayer. This eternal cycle is the secret of continued progress, eternal expansion, and infinite satisfaction. If we fervently pray, we'll find an unending future of discoveries about God and unlimited growth.

Spiritual Alchemy

The secret of this fantastic inner transformation is the personal spirit guide in each of us that provides intimate contact with the Creator. The phenomenon of the creature touching the Creator, of the human and divine holding each other, is the core of The Universal Spiritual Way and provides all the miracles of spiritual transformation. We give the voice and touch of God a doorway which widens as we increase our commitment to know and do His will.

The value and ecstasy of the Universal Father's touch is based on personal interaction. Compare experiences: hugging a tree or hugging your daughter, gripping the steering wheel or gently holding your lover's hand, pushing the 34th floor button or pushing a child on a swing, anguishing to the sky or sobbing with a friend, total focus on career or complete devotion to family.

The supreme joys of life are those times we touch others. If the mystery and genuineness of heart-to-heart sharing with family, friends, and others is supportive and breathtaking, just imagine what we achieve through sincere prayer and inner-worship—our hearts *directly* touching God's. The Creator delights when we come to Him, meeting his spirit through inner-worship.

When we give all to contact with the Creator, utterly open our hearts past the layers of mind, we sing through the soul and have an immediate, personal encounter, a divine embrace. We worship the First Source and Center, the Creator, the Protector, the Infinite Upholder, The Universal Father.

Though God has countless universe beings seeking His attention and guidance, though He must uphold and control the universe from the eternal past, present, and future, though you are human and imperfect, despite what you've done or will do (God knows the future), your loving heavenly Father is always open and desires to give you His touch NOW. Nothing can stop the Creator's affection for you or change your real desire for Him. It's up to you.

> For I am persuaded, that neither death, nor life, nor angels, nor principalities, nor powers, nor things present, nor things to come,
>
> Nor height, nor depth, nor any other creature, shall be able to separate us from the love of God . . .
>
> —Romans 8:38-39, *The Bible*

Let's stop for a minute . . . Do we really comprehend what's being offered from God? What if I said you were invited to a good friend's home for dinner, how would you feel? Probably good. If you're happily partnered or married, what would it be like to spend a week alone in a romantic spot? If you're single, how about finding your dream mate? Imagine seeing children, relatives, or friends after a long separation. *Feel the elation.* Consider meeting a famous person you admire—quite a thrill.

Now . . . believe and realize that the Creator of these people and yourself is always available and provides friendship and intimacy beyond measure. Let it sink in . . . God loves you—

child of the cosmos—and wants to give you a way to have direct contact with him. All that's needed is your acceptance of and investment in your inner God experience.

Want to know this reality? Haven't been here before? Feeling awkward and unpracticed, a bit unworthy? Remember, all you have to do is pray with sincerity, intensity, and with regularity. Period. God puts no restrictions on His love for and contact with you. He's hoping (as I write) that I can inspire you to pray. He's waiting for you and me to pray: it's the first step.

Open the door of your being with profound prayer. Enlarge your capacity to receive unlimited energy. *Supercharge your soul.*

More effective than, tithing, incense, candles, reading, listening to lectures, study, going to conferences, church, meditating, dancing, astrology, philosophy, science, social activism, exercise, socializing, self-pity, counseling, or self-help, the simple, quiet act of being alone with and talking to God with faith is the surest way to peace, assurance, divine certainty, and happiness.

Although we embellish and many times avoid prayer, nothing is more primal, basic, or effective for making contact with God. All spiritual experience and moral achievement is based on it.

Our slumbering personal spiritual potential is released when the door is opened. Wholehearted dedication to profound prayer opens and then steadily enlarges the sparkling, refreshing stream from the divine to the human. Prayer actually expands our being, like ripples from a stone thrown in a lake. If we don't make an effort, we may only get a tiny, incidental drip. But, when we open our hearts (clear the pipes), back comes the rush of divine power and nourishment that actually and literally enlarges our celestial plumbing—the spiritual reception capacity.

So, let's believe and understand that contact with God does all. There's nothing that God asks us to become or do that outdistances His quick and transforming love; Nothing is really impossible if He wills it, especially when it's the reclamation and eternalization of His earth children.

God provides all and delivers the fruits. It's up to us.

The Fruits of the Spirit

It's reassuring and very comforting to think about how God can transform us. But, to find better, more meaningful and joyful lives, we have to strive and sweat. The real test for your prayer life is that it should stimulate you to action and bring real growth and soul expansion. This is the greatest treasure of all, the pearl of great price.

How many millions of words have we read? How many long, interesting talks have we listened to? How many videos, podcasts, groups, shows, and books have we experienced? Now. Here. *Let's vault over fear and complacency to celebrate and use the gifts laid at our feet.*

After all, if we've experienced and welcomed the truth that we're children of The Universal Father and are one family, and if we've acknowledged God's process to help us transcend our personal limitations, if we believe, then God expects us to *do something*, to live from the celebrated foundations he provides. When you know with peace, assurance, and security that God's will can bring the best for you and all humankind, the next step is to *be* a dynamic agent and promoter of that Plan.

We're required to become spiritual adults once we've entered the new world. We're expected to show the fruits of the Spirit. Now the joyful, strenuous, eternally-rewarding work begins.

God brings us unconditional help and understanding but also an intense urgency to our decisions. He requires our increasing devotion and self-forgetfulness. Although we may sincerely contact God anytime, fulfilling progress and expansion require *dynamic devotion* to God. Our loving Divine Father expects us to yield increasing benefits for others and ourselves by intently, resolutely, and unreservedly trying to follow His guidance.

The glories of spiritual realization lead to stronger and more focused service paths and dedication to spiritual practice, bringing us up the magic spiral of celestial accomplishment.

God wants us to be successful, to achieve, build, inspire, risk, serve, spread, grow, activate, slingshot, propel, run, be persistent, be comforting, lay it on the line, share, stand up tall, speak the truth, cooperate, facilitate, be patient, be disciplined, enforce, uphold, strengthen, induce, push the envelope, stretch the soul, and reach for the stars.

The Father welcomes and cheers us to be powerful instruments of His eternal and absolute design for total universe achievement of matter, mind, and spirit. What adventure, mystery, activity, pursuit, or goal is more fantastic and worthy than complete personal growth? We must remember!

> There is a space between man's imagination and man's attainment that may only be traversed by his longing.
>
> —Kahlil Gibran, *Sand and Foam*

The benefits of divine actualization—Spirit fruits—only occur when we *risk everything* in total embrace of the Creator's will. We must make God's will the overarching priority that unifies and determines other priorities. We must use this approach: "If God wants me to do something, I'll do it. If my course of action isn't in accord with God's will, I'll alter it."

The highest prayer is: IT IS MY WILL THAT YOUR WILL BE DONE. In fact, the *only* gift we can bring to God is the consecration of our will to follow Him. The endless quantity and variety of spiritual benefits flowing from infinity are only realized when we try to know and follow God's leading.

The perfect standard of all spiritual and religious thought is this: Are you willing to do God's will in any circumstance, despite all consequences? Is your life flowing with the characteristics of the Spirit? Do you bear fruit? Does your prayer and the life it creates bring you closer to God and God closer to you? Simply, do you pray to do God's will? Is your love increasing for others?

So, as we move along in this book, let's keep this standard in mind, accepting that it's the basis for the fruits of the Spirit we desire. When you thrill and admire spiritual achievements, understand that the only way to achieve them is by a valid prayer process: inner-worship of God, and *action.*

Yes, we're challenged and sometimes overwhelmed with life but are invited to participate in the most stunning, satisfying, and privileged universe event. We're children of God and should be overjoyed and tingle with unbounded anticipation and sweet curiosity for the pageant of divine creation. The keys are here, always the same.

Again, the secret—the bull's eye—is sincere heart-chosen attitudes: hunger for the truth, faith acceptance action, courage, and hard work. To feel and reflect the spiritual truths, we must wholeheartedly and sincerely seek and accept them, acting with faith to do the Father's will. We serve others by understanding forgiveness and love, the eternal standard and axiom of The Universal Spiritual Way.

Earlier, we discussed the power of the Spirit when it touches the heart and attitude area—the center of the target. Now it's time to go out one more circle from the center and examine the benefits to the mind. It's the mind where most of us invest the bulk of our time dealing with daily demands, thinking about the past, and hoping for the future. Unfortunately, we seldom cultivate relaxation and are gripped by incessant thought and stimulation: home, family, the phone, the car, the wash, shopping, etc.

But, when we make room for the Spirit, our minds are refreshed and allowed to achieve what's beyond their conception.

The Spirit's caress brings wonderful rest, which enables insight, clear thinking, stability, and creative adaptation. The Spirit's impact fosters superb mental health and a realization that we're not alone, that we're indwelt by God's helper who is with us in all circumstances.

Consequently, when we encounter trying days, which demand more than we can provide, there's a pure reservoir waiting to be used. By intensely asking for help and communing with God, we immediately experience gradual peace, improved insight and logic, and the certainty that someone is going to be with us until the end. Gnawing isolation is soothed with companionship, constant encouragement, and inspiration from the Spirit within you.

Prayer comforts and heals every wound. But, that's just the beginning. Prayer inspires and empowers us.

Our minds often rebel against what we know we need to do. Although we might approach a necessary task with apathy, boredom, or dread, by surrendering our minds to God we're rescued from the laziness, and we stop our whining and get to work. Our minds become resolute and unified, using all thought and emotion to get the job done without thinking of self.

It's that overemphasis of self—What's in it for me? When will I be done?—that drains the stores of spiritual ambition and mind power. When we desire to serve and freely forget our egos, we swim with the stream, get used to the temperature, and quickly make progress. Liaison with the Spirit is the key.

And sometimes, we just think too much. Like the physical strain of over-exercise, our minds begin to ache and are soon depleted. New ideas disappear and we have trouble with what used to be simple problems. It becomes very difficult to draw on our experiences and wisdom; we get limp and *depressed.* But, by resting in prayer and inner-worship, we give God room to till the soil, weed, and water our gardens.

The Spirit within brings superb mental health and quickens the decisions that lead there, whether it be talking to a spouse, getting medication, seeing a therapist, or changing careers. God highlights our highest ideals and values, which in turn enable us to go in the right direction. Most critical, he gives us the self-respect of being His children.

We've been told we shouldn't judge ourselves by other's standards, but by our own. But, remember that the most objective perspective is from God: *It's more important to listen to what God thinks of you than what you think of yourself.*

What a relief!

But, more important than better thoughts, God changes our inner qualities. The most impressive measure, the greatest achievement of self, is character, revealed in our decisions and behavior. Everyone's seen people who say the right things but are unwilling to uphold what they believe or admire. These people can be quite sophisticated and "learned," often having enviable material and professional success, but unwilling to release and live in their souls they forego real riches. Heart is the key.

Our actions are shaped by our animal minds or our eternal souls. When we act unconsciously from the gut, we are pawns of circumstance and environment. However, when we decide to put ourselves in our souls, then all the wonderful characteristics (those things we admire in human nature) begin to emerge and flower.

Take any quality: loyalty, forgiveness, tolerance, mercy, honesty, hope, steadfastness, etc., and realize that it's a spiritual reaction superseding the mind and coming from the soul. The more we pray and commune, the more we will enjoy the most important Spirit fruits and realize, as children of God, stabilizing self-respect.

The true spiritual desires of the soul burn brighter in our minds and replace or transform our purely self-centered, animal urges and needs. And when we dare to pursue the spiritual, when we dare to think in new ways, God's spirit transforms our minds and gives us unlimited energy for real spiritual action to change our lives.

These personal tendencies and reaction habits form the basis for all that's true, beautiful, and good, as well as provide the most satisfaction and accomplishment to the doer. The easiest way to record your progress is to describe your actions. Are you manifesting more and more inner light or avoiding total commitment? Do you take time to understand, love, and serve those you know? How would an objective observer describe your actions?

If we're excited and motivated to spread the truth of The Universal Spiritual Way, we need to remember that the best way to get people to listen is by *manifesting Spirit fruits.* If we live such a well-balanced life, between the needs of the mind, body, and soul, then people will be drawn to us and listen. Eventually, we'll achieve total self-mastery. We'll put God first and be willing to do anything to achieve His will and support the spiritual life. ALL.

> Father in Heaven! It is from Thy hand that we receive all. Thou stretchest forth Thy powerful hand and it seizes the wise in their foolishness; Thou stretchest forth Thy powerful hand and worlds pass away. Thou openest Thy compassionate hand and it fills with abundant blessing all that live, and if at times Thou seemest to take Thy hand from us, we know that Thou dost only close it in order to conceal a blessing yet more abundant. We know that Thou dost only close Thy hand in order to open it again and to fill abundantly with blessing all who live.
>
> —Soren Kierkegaard, *The Prayers of Kierkegaard*

The Greatest Blessing

As we look at the benefits of prayer, the most important point is that prayer allows us to overcome all limitations of heart-attitude, mind, and soul. These aspects of self, these parts of the human target, are wonderful, but we must also accept that they're limited, not powerful enough.

Instead of feeling disappointed, we should be glad at the opportunity to grow: Dissatisfaction is the origin of the growth desire. Problems are true allies sending us out to discover and cooperate with God to create new capacities in all parts of our being. This is the greatest miracle—personal spiritual alchemy.

If you need will-power and motivation, better or new attitudes, improved thought, self-control and mastery, soul revelations, better prayer and worship, or don't quite know, understand that *prayer and inner-worship of God brings all the power you need to change yourself.* Whatever inner reserves and energy you need in any area, if it's in accord with God's will, you will get it, eventually.

Our hearts are soon bathed in God's supreme embrace and erupt in gigantic, ever-expanding waves of jubilation, celebration, success, service, love, thankfulness, and total confidence. All needs are fulfilled. Our talents and spiritual potentials are expanded by cooperating with our Maker.

Honestly, can any hurt, deficiency of character, or situation defeat us, the human children of the One, the Maker, the Planner, the Source, our loving Father? Nothing can stop us if we accept God and let Him open our hearts and talents, if we work hard every day to follow His gracious leading.

If the capacities of our minds and souls determine our potential range of responses to life, then when God repeatedly enlarges them he enables even broader, improved varieties of spiritual responses and fruits of the spirit.

There are no limits on your growth or destiny. Limitations—anything that impairs the realization of your natural gifts and spiritual reactions—like death, disease, time, confusion, and character flaws, are preludes to divine assurance for solid growth, total spiritual fulfillment, infinite revelation, and eternal life.

You are a child of a good, wise Divine Parent.

This may be difficult to accept when you're faced with real world challenges or if you had inadequate or bad parents. But, please be brave (prayer for courage) and remember that benefits only happen when you try to give absolute, wholehearted, self-forgetful prayer for help and knowledge of God's will, accepting the truths God will reveal about Himself and your life.

Don't let the bad experiences or your misconceptions rob you of your eternal heritage any longer!

Shut off your mind for a while every day and commune with God. Your loving Parent wants you to know joyful realization of your status as His beloved child and to continually celebrate spiritual, intellectual, and material achievement. Accept who you are!

When you accept God within and work on that relationship, you get phenomenal self-respect and Spirit qualities: You're empowered to harmoniously reach out to preserve and improve family, friendship, community, and any group based on worthy goals. Groups benefit from the Spirit to the extent that their members dedicate themselves to the Spirit.

Groups with a high service vision become illuminated and improved as their members see their personal ideals elevated in the group. Prayer begins to solidify groups around God's will and promotes selflessness, self-restraint, and progress. It is the ideal socializing, moralizing, and spiritualizing influence. All Spirit-led groups, while having different beliefs, have goals, that when combined, achieve God's will.

People don't have to think alike to have true spiritual unity. If we are led by God, our differences of opinion provide variety for the best path to fulfill God's ultimate plan here on earth. When we all follow God, we're willing to accept his authority and guidance and compromise with others to heal wounds and make progress. Without mutual acceptance of One God, there is no peace.

Just as God has a plan for you, work that only you can do, He has plans for groups, work that only they can do. There's no more effective group than one that's unified under a sublime service goal and sustained by fervent personal and collective prayer. As our world eventually becomes spiritual, more groups will function this way and bond to encompass all humankind under the common vision of the Brotherhood of Man. They will realize all the benefits of prayer—every fruit of the Spirit.

These beliefs may seem unreasonable or over-optimistic, but when we accept the truths about God, we transcend the animal nature and see eternal visions. We embrace The Universal Spiritual Way. What's impossible for our minds becomes the soul's habit. It's only through willingness (as an unspoiled child) to reach our true spiritual ideals that we'll have any success in changing ourselves and our world.

It's only by elevating the mind through prayer and inner-worship of God that we can transcend it and see that what we thought was impossible, is really spiritually possible: We use our thoughts to achieve the ideals that our souls reveal to us. Let's celebrate the fruits and the life that makes these goals possible and dedicate ourselves to effective prayer.

Never forget your divine heritage. Even as you know where to find your favorite music or food, celebrate the fact that your greatest gifts are present, accessible, and INSIDE. Stop. Drink in this thought with belief and complete faith. Dump misdirection and decay. Strengthen your life. Pray that you always remember that you are a child of God. Find the fruits of the spirit.

Pray at a profound level.

Spiritual Truths

Problems are necessary for improvement.

Only belief in the truths about God can lead us to progress.

Prayer is the most effective tool for growth,
born from soul longing.

Prayer improves attitude.

The Spirit within supplies power and love directly
from the Father.

Prayer brings improvement in mind function.

Our personal characteristics improve with prayer.

Prayer enables us to overcome all limitations of heart and mind.

Part II

The Essentials of Prayer

When we pray, we link ourselves with the inexhaustible power that spins the universe. We ask that a part of this power be apportioned to our needs. Even in asking, our human deficiencies are filled and we arise, strengthened and repaired.

—Alexis Carrel, *Readers Digest*, March 1941

How to Pray

The Keys to Divine Dialogue

Chapter 4

In New York City in the early 1800s, it was quite a challenge to get from Brooklyn to Manhattan Island. The only way was to take a ferry, and that could be dangerous. The Brooklyn Bridge solved this problem when it opened in 1883 after fourteen years of painstaking design and careful construction. It was the vision of John Augustus Roebling, accomplished through many personal sacrifices by his son, Washington Roebling, and his wife, Emily Warren Roebling. The workers on the bridge also paid a very heavy price with scores of injuries and almost thirty deaths.

Yet, the bridge was an incredible, unprecedented success and is a beautiful, life-giving landmark today. It became the model for new bridge designs, solving transportation problems across the world. But most importantly, it greatly improved life for people living in Brooklyn and Manhattan and stimulated tremendous growth and opportunity at each end of the bridge. The key to its success was vision, drive, innovation, organization, risk, and dedication.

Those are the same ingredients we need in our spiritual lives. If we want to make progress, we must focus, commit, work, change, fall down, get up, try again, and celebrate. And, sustaining this upward spiral requires regular, daily, effective praying. It requires a continuous supply of power from inner-worship as well.

Prayer is the indispensable key to all spiritual progress, and in this chapter we'll look at how to pray to find peace, assurance, security, and power.

The Nature of Prayer

Prayer is a conversation—communication with God. Like any conversation, one person starts, the other person listens, then responds. Since the eternal Father placed His spirit in each of us, he longs for conversation with us. God wants to be our true friend, a part of every struggle in our lives, always there to help us change with the power of eternity.

God really wants to be your best friend and has a unique destiny for you. Prayer will help you find that destiny a little more each day as you talk more with God and discover His will for your life. The key to spiritual success, and prayer, is to discover and do your best to follow the leading from the Father's spirit within you. When you dedicate yourself to following God's guidance, His desires eventually come to pass in your life. Sooner or later, His will IS. And, this is the best possible future you could have. When you desire the Father's will and try to follow it, *no power in the universe can stop you.*

Our Father who is in heaven,
Hallowed be your name.
Your kingdom come, your will be done,
On earth as it is in heaven.
Give us this day our bread for tomorrow;
Refresh our souls with the water of life.
And forgive us every one our debts,
As we also have forgiven our debtors.
Save us in temptation, deliver us from evil,
And increasingly make us perfect like yourself.

—Jesus, from *The Urantia Book*

So, true prayer is a process of growing by aligning our will to God's. *True prayer is a process to transform ourselves,* not to fulfill material desires or ask for certain outcomes in our lives or in the world. True prayer helps us discover new values and ideals and always leads to a deeper relationship with God. *The purpose of prayer is to transform us*; it is not to change God's decisions. This allows us to transcend our limitations in order to see and live in the world as God does.

Every prayer that sincerely asks for spiritual growth for ourselves or others is heard by God. Every prayer that's made from a real spiritual motivation will flash directly to God's mind. But, every prayer that has a different motivation will not be heard. Prayers for vengeance, material wealth, power, and ease, are heavy, material-minded thoughts that can never ascend the fresh air to God's heights.

So, words make no difference in prayer. You could have the most beautiful, poetic phrases, but if you're not sincere, if you're putting on a show to assure yourself or gain the approval of others, you're deluded if you think you're going to change God or that God will even hear what you're saying. You'll live in a dream-world of your own making instead of the matchless real world that God has for you.

Just as relaxation and meditation prepare us for prayer, prayer is the gateway to expressing nothing but appreciation and adoration toward God: This is the state of true inner-worship where our souls are fully engaged in communion with the Father of Lights. It's a sanctuary within where we don't ask for anything but immerse ourselves in the Divine Father's love and express our total thankfulness. There is no self-interest, there is no asking, there is only giving our love back to God and accepting.

This is where we are nourished and supercharged, in the inner-worship of God. How else could we receive the matchless, infinite power of the Creator? Where could we find a better source?

True prayer relies on continual belief-acceptance of the foundational truths of The Universal Spiritual Way: You a child of God. We are family. Eternal progress is yours through faith acceptance and the living of these truths. Real prayer is enabled by having the wholehearted faith-acceptance and trust of a child as well as total sincerity and a hunger for truth.

Real prayer is the positive reaction to all challenges and all problems in life. Even though we may become discouraged and saddened at times, real prayer is the conduit of light, power, and God's love, sustaining us through our growth into better tomorrows.

Real prayer is the process of transcending ourselves to make seemingly impossible personal changes. Real prayer is the fulcrum that helps us imitate and become more like God. Real prayer is the gateway to unlimited spiritual nourishment in the sublime experience of inner-worship of the Creator.

Real prayer is the best tool we could have from our best friend—God. Real prayer should be nurtured and is the most important activity of our day. Real prayer is the gateway to the divine in our every day and the prelude to eternity.

But, real prayer is only possible if we make room for it.

Giving Prayer a Home

If you want to create something lasting and beautiful, you have to be committed. If you want to have effective prayer, you have to make time for it and provide the best environment possible in your circumstances. Of course, you can pray any time you want, but to enter a state of altered consciousness with the Creator, you need to make the best arrangements for prayer. If you want to gain as much inspiration and comfort as you can, if you want to find real power to solve your real problems, you need to create a regular place for sustained contact with God.

Just think of anything created by humans that you admire; any achievement in your life that you cherish. Every one of these accomplishments took focus and commitment; Prayer is no different. If we want effective prayer, we need to be very focused and willing to do what's necessary.

> As long as we are persistent in the pursuit of our deepest destiny, we will continue to grow. We cannot choose the day or time when we will fully bloom. It happens in its own time.
>
> —Denis Waitley

This means that if we want to see the benefits of prayer, we have to make it a very high priority. We have to set aside time each day and stop doing some of the things we've been doing. The only way to get more time for prayer is to give less time to other things.

So, when you start your day, are there some things that you do that you really don't need to do, that you can spend less time doing, or that you can do at another time? When we start to remove the clutter—the things that we thought were important—we find more than enough time to do the things that are truly of spiritual value.

The time we put into prayer provides tremendous benefits that empower us to do even more, ultimately resulting in saving us time. Because we have more power, we're more effective and things take less time. Not only do we have more power, but prayer helps us focus and clean out even more of the clutter that's in the way of living a truly free, liberated spiritual life.

We need to take a very serious look at everything if we're going to determine what's helping us or helping others grow closer to God and live more fulfilling spiritual lives. If what you're doing doesn't bring you or others closer to God, then it should be a lower priority. In the end, *the only thing we take with us is our souls*, and those are created by following God's lead.

Most often, the things that compete with prayer are just ordinary activities—nothing sinister. Just think of everything that pecks away at our time: email, texts, phone calls, the Internet, videos, blogs, books, music, radio, television, newspapers, magazines, billboards, electronic devices, and all the little activities that we *think* we need to do every day. If you add them all up, their power is constant, enormous, addicting.

This doesn't mean that we should cut out everything that we enjoy doing and that everything you do during your day has to have profound spiritual meaning. But we need to put the spiritual things first and be willing to do less of the other activities. We need to follow spiritual stars, not lust after material things or power. The only way to find a new spiritual life is through spiritual rebirth and then dedication to God's will through regular prayer, inner-worship, and service to others.

We have to stop doing and thinking some things, and do and think others much, much, much more. The material focus should be transformed into the spiritual focus.

True happiness, peace, assurance, security, and joy, is found in spiritual growth activities. And, prayer is the most effective activity to create this future.

You really have to think of yourself as a spiritual athlete. When you look at what makes an athlete successful, it's many of the same things that make spiritual progress possible. You and I, as often as we can, for as long as we can, need to remind ourselves of the purpose of life: spiritual growth. We should be willing to reprioritize the activities in our lives, to organize our days to find time and make a real home for prayer. We need to be willing to keep putting out effort over and over again. We need to take prayer seriously.

> The prayer offered to God in the morning during your quiet time is the key that unlocks the door of the day. Any athlete knows that it is the start that ensures a good finish.
>
> —Adrian Rogers

But, this doesn't mean that we can't be spontaneous and playful with our spiritual lives. God doesn't want us to be robots. After all, God wants us to be happy. He wants us to delight in all the pleasures of life but to make spiritual progress the highest priority. He wants us to make service to others the highest priority.

So, as we start to think about how to make a home for prayer, please remember that you can pray at any time, in any place, under any circumstances. I'm just saying, that to have the most effective, the deepest, the most beneficial prayer, you need to be determined to create good places and regular, significant times for prayer, for being alone with God.

The first step is to look at your daily schedule and not try to do too much prayer to begin with. Remember that small steps—incremental progress—have the best chance of lasting. I suggest that you start by scheduling a time each day that you'll pray. This doesn't have to be the only time you pray, but, this scheduled time is the seed that can grow into a sustained, life-giving practice.

So, when you wake to start your day, pray right away. I won't say for how long, but it's best to start out slowly and follow your soul's desires. Make time to recognize the soul's attitudes, desires, and longings so you can express them through prayer.

One of the things you should pray for, near the end of your prayers, is for the desire to pray again. When you do this, you're building a bridge to the next life-giving conversation with God, this day, or the next. You're creating life-giving, nourishing spiritual habits to truly transform your life. This can be an eternal, life-giving circle.

There's no other way to progress. But, that's not all you must do.

It's good to have regular times to pray, but you have to do it in a good environment, in private. So, think about a place in your home where you can be alone. This may be difficult to find, but if you really try, you'll most likely be able to find a place at some time where you can be alone in prayer with God. And, if you can't find a place at home for this, look for a place outside of your home, in nature, in a sacred place.

If you're living a spiritual life, if you have spiritual goals, you most likely have family or friends on a spiritual path. See if they'd be interested in praying with you. See if they'd be interested in gathering to pray. Even though it's critical that you form your own spiritual relationship with God and pray alone, it's also critical that you find people who are on the same path who can sustain, inspire, and support you and would be willing to join you in group prayer.

Yes, this book is about profound praying to transcend old misconceptions and limitations, to find a direct experience of God. But, it doesn't mean that you shouldn't seek out spiritual community. It doesn't mean that you shouldn't attend a church. But, it does mean that you should find a spiritual community, church, temple, synagogue, mosque, etc., that's dedicated to following God's leading and will help you to grow and find your own interpretation of the truth and divine will.

And, to have the most effective power for growth, we need to have effective prayer. To be true spiritual athletes, we need to do what works.

The Prayer Recipe

Effective prayer starts with *wholehearted* belief in the basic spiritual truths: You are a child of a loving divine parent and we're family. He'll give you everything you need and you can create an eternal future by using your faith and following His guidance. These are the core truths of The Universal Spiritual

Way. It's the gateway to effective prayer and a completely new world.

So, when you're praying, remember these essential truths and express your sincere longing to find more truth and become a better person. Express the desires of your soul. *Pour out your heart to God as intensely as you can, for as long as you can, as often as you can.* Share your sincere desire to grow. Come with the attitude of a trusting, secure child. Accept. Believe the inner love-embrace from God. Use this faith to unlock the treasures of prayer.

Wholehearted sincerity, a hunger for the truth, and acceptance of faith enables us to find the truth and God's guidance, and is the foundation of effective prayer.

As you're confronted by challenges, remember to pray every day and not be discouraged. Remember the peace, assurance, and security from your Divine Father and know that no outside force can really harm your relationship with God or your spiritual destiny. Events may be dark, painful, and confusing, but if you nourish yourself with the divine embrace, you'll realize that you can be an invincible, growing child of God. *No force in the universe can stop you from realizing your destiny*, if you dedicate yourself to finding and following God's guidance.

God's eternal plan can't be stopped.

If we accept that we're on an eternal journey of growth and discovery, if we accept that the purpose of life is to grow spiritually, then the greatest joys in life are in growth and giving to others: We realize that the focus of prayer is to help us grow. When you pray, pray for growth. Pray that God transforms your attitudes and your thoughts and gives you the power to live as he would live in your life circumstances.

If we're focused on growth, then challenges and problems are opportunities, necessities for growth. We don't grow without challenges; we don't grow without problems. we don't grow without stretching.

Some people say that God never gives you more than you can handle. But, actually, *God does give you more than you can handle* so you will ask for help and then grow. And, the way we fill the gap between what we're capable of doing and what God has challenged us to do, is through sincere and regular prayer and inner-worship of God—the ultimate doorway to transformation.

> Ask and it shall be given you; seek and you will find; knock and it shall be opened to you. For every one who asks receives; he who seeks finds; and to him who knocks the door of salvation will be opened.
>
> —Jesus, from *The Urantia Book*

Use prayer as a way to solve problems. Pray for personal transformation. Don't pray for things. Pray to become more like God. It's only then that you'll find true, undreamed-of happiness.

When you come to God in prayer, remember to use the matchless foundation of complete trust in God. Come to God with total acceptance of the divine inner experience, with total, believing faith. Remember to be persistent. Don't expect instant change or instant answers. When you fall down, get up and try again with God. Keep trusting and asking God to transform you. Keep asking God to help others and to help you help them as well.

God will give you everything you need when you need it, in the way you need it, for as long as you need it. If you're not ready for the kind of spiritual change that you're praying for, God will gently lead you to change, step by step at the right time.

Before you even come to prayer, be sure that you're courageously doing *everything you can* to tackle the problem or challenge in front of you. It's only when you're doing everything you possibly can to meet a challenge that you're able to open your heart completely to the Father's transforming spirit. Faith, courage, and persistent hard work are as important to personal transformation as wind is to a sailboat.

Things just don't happen because you want them to happen or visualize them. Spiritual evolution is a divine technique made possible by the eternal potentials from God and from our **persistent effort**: You must work hard in the outer world.

When we believe that we're children of a perfect, loving, Divine Father, then we're accepting the inner experience of God. Soon, through prayer, we experience more and more of God and feel increasing peace, assurance, security, and power. So, when you pray, remember that Father-God experience and surrender all desires to the transforming power of God within. Give your total trust to where God's leading you.

> It seems to us that the will of God bends when our prayer is heard and granted; yet it is our will alone that ascends. We begin to will in time what God has willed us from all eternity.
>
> —Reginald Garrigou-Lagrange,
> *Christian Perfection and Contemplation*

As you pray more and more, as you start to touch the experience of inner-worship, you'll begin to understand what God wants you to do. And, as you do, remember to pray to find and understand God's will even more and to make the only purpose of your life to follow His leading. If you trust God completely, you know that by following His will you'll find the best possible future for yourself and others, that you'll find an experience more wonderful and fulfilling than anything you could imagine.

Pray each day to follow God. Try to do His will. Pray again and again and again to know and understand the clear light.

And, be sure to pray for others. Don't pray too much for yourself. Pray that the people in your life will experience God more and respond to Him. Pray for their spiritual growth and the power for them to face their life challenges with faith and hope. When you find yourself being critical of another person, be sure to pray for them. Tell them you're praying for them and be sure not to avoid them in your life.

Be tactful and understanding, not condescending or proud. Set the tone of a true friend, not someone who is superior and has all the answers. When you're led by God, make close contact with others and try to help them.

But, be careful in the way you tell someone you're praying for them, especially if they don't have the same spiritual beliefs as you. You don't want them to get the feeling that you think you're superior or special, or judging or requiring them to change their beliefs. This is most important with people who are atheists or just aren't sure about God or had a bad experience with a spiritual group.

When you pray, realize that God is meeting all your spiritual needs and knows them even before you think of asking. God sees the future and has already arranged every opportunity for spiritual growth that you'll need through eternity. Pray intelligently. Trust and pray for the right things and be transported to the real world of God.

Come to God and share all your challenges and needs. Pray most of all for:

1. Knowledge of God's specific guidance for you
2. Wisdom for making basic decisions in your daily life
3. Spiritual progress for your family and friends
4. The gifts, the fruits of the Spirit
5. Those who hurt you
6. The growth of God's influence in the hearts of His children
7. The desire to pray again

Most importantly, ask God to help you pray more often and more effectively. Ask God to help you purify your heart and amplify your hunger for truth and faith-acceptance of the light within. Ask him to make the desires from your eternal soul grow stronger and clearer. Always ask God to help you pray again and again, to keep the cycle of spiritual nourishment progressing.

Learning When and How to Listen

Traditionally, many people who are part of an organized religion think they need to rely on an intermediary or middleman for themselves and God. They often view God as a distant cosmic force or an old father with a flowing beard, a stern taskmaster or authority figure, quick to judge the smallest fault, and quick to punish. At the very least, many people view God as a distant, profound mystery—more of a concept than a person.

But, the truth is that a unique peace of the Creator of the universe lives within you and wants to know you one-to-one. God wants you to respond to His loving touch and begin a friendship that will last for eternity, to nourish the most important friendship of your life. And prayer is the most basic part of this friendship. Prayer is simply, conversation with God.

Since God is a real person, the source of all people, it's really possible to have a relationship with Him. We can feel God and share our thoughts and longings with Him; he can touch us, he can communicate with us. The Eternal Father is working with you to achieve your truest spiritual longings and desires which he has placed there. God really is your best friend.

This means that the things we've learned in our basic human friendships apply in many ways to our friendship with God. You have to spend time with your friends. You need to be interested in your friends. You need to listen to your friends. You need to try to help your friends with their challenges. You need to have fun together. You need to share your life together. And you need to share your hearts with each other, even if it means an uncomfortable exchange. Most of all, you need to help each other.

Believe it or not, God really does need your help. There is a profound and unique reason that you were created since you have a profound and unique personality and set of gifts. God placed you in your position in life so that you may know the greatest spiritual joy and make the biggest contribution to His divine plan with your unique destiny path. When we achieve, when we follow the Father's will, we help God, we serve God: *The only gift we can give God is our cooperation with His plan.*

> It is better to strive in one's own dharma than to succeed in the dharma of another. Nothing is ever lost in following one's own dharma, but competition in another's dharma breeds fear and insecurity.
>
> —*The Bhagavad Gita*

These truths grow out of the essential truths of The Universal Spiritual Way. Prayer that's based on these truths is far different than other types of prayer.

Many people only come to God when they need something or in a pressing situation. Many people only come to God when they want God to change something in their lives or in the world for them. But if we accept the liberating truths of The Universal Spiritual Way, we realize that prayer is a profound opportunity to grow and is a real conversation with God, not a one-way communication of us sharing our wish list.

So, when you get done pouring out your heart to God, when you get done asking God to help you and others grow, it's time to listen to God.

Try imagining a conversation where only one person talks for an extended period of time. Have you ever been on the receiving end of this kind of experience? It doesn't feel like a friendship, does it? So, why should it be any different with God?

When we pray we need to remember to pause and listen to God. After we get done sharing are concerns, longings, hopes and dreams, we need to let God share His hopes and dreams for us. Any good conversation is a natural rhythm, and we should practice this art with God.

Once you've had your say, sit in silence and let yourself experience what God's sharing with you. Give this some time. *Don't expect quick results.* At first you may feel nothing, but please know that each time you pray, and then listen, you're making steady progress: You'll begin to feel increasing peace, assurance, and security.

Then, with all your heart, say how much you appreciate God and what He has given you. Enter the realm of inner-worship and don't expect or ask for anything. Sing with your inner-voice with complete thankfulness to Him. Sit quietly and listen and begin again. Say how much you adore and love God. Listen. Do this over and over until your soul is satisfied in this perfect expression of inner-worship of God. Listen to His guidance and promise to do your best to follow it.

In time, your prayer and worship with God will change because you're changing; You're making it possible for God to share more with you. When we're born, it's virtually impossible for us to communicate with our parents, but, things gradually change. Minute by minute, hour by hour, day by day, as we interact more and more with our parents, we learn to communicate; we learn what a family is. Most of all, we learn who we are and how we can contribute the most to the family.

Our spiritual evolution is very, very similar. Just expect that this is a slow but dependable process. If God wanted us to be perfect now, he would've created us that way. Instead, he's given us the transforming gift of evolution so that we may have the thrill of achievement and self-transformation to perfection.

Don't expect fantastic signs, messages, or phenomena during prayer or inner-worship; don't expect to be given very detailed instructions or spectacular revelations. These things can happen, but they're in no way a part of the usual prayer and inner-worship experience.

That's why we have to be very, very careful with evaluating what we think is inner guidance, or what we think that guidance is saying to us. This is especially true in the beginning of our prayer life.

When you have a question for God, when you're asking for God's advice, don't expect to get all the answers at once. Be persistent, and ask God again and again, every day, every week, for the guidance you seek. Eventually, you'll get that inner assurance and embrace of divine love that validates and clarifies God's guidance.

Welcome this process and be willing to let go of everything that's preventing or slowing down your spiritual growth. Be willing to pray at a profound level, beyond any human organization or middleman.

Spiritual Truths

The only gift we can give God is to do His will.

Sincerity, truth hunger, faith, and wholeheartedness are the foundation of prayer.

The purpose of real prayer is for growth and the power to grow.

Spiritual nourishment is dependent on deep, regular, solitary, quality prayer and inner-worship with God.

Effective prayer is dependent on doing all we can to meet challenges.

Effective prayer requires total surrender to God's guidance.

Prayer should not only be for one's self but for others as well.

True prayer is a natural part of friendship with God.

No prayer can be ethical when the petitioner seeks for selfish advantage over his fellows. Selfish and materialistic praying is incompatible with the ethical religions which are predicated on unselfish and divine love. All such unethical praying reverts to the primitive levels of pseudo magic and is unworthy of advancing civilizations and enlightened religions. Selfish praying transgresses the spirit of all ethics founded on loving justice.

Prayer must never be so prostituted as to become a substitute for action. All ethical praying is a stimulus to action and a guide to the progressive striving for idealistic goals of super self-attainment.

—*The Urantia Book*

Prayer Killers

The Poisons to Prayer

Chapter 5

My family and I live in the Northeastern part of the United States and have a fairly lush yard—most of it not by design. We have a few hundred-foot oak trees, various bushes, other types of flora, and a lawn. Over the past twenty years, I've tried again and again to improve the lawn, usually with environmental methods.

I've brought in new soil, filled in swampy areas, watered, removed weeds by hand, raked, used an electric mower, hand-dug a drainage system, and reduced flooding. The results are mixed, but we still have a very pleasant place to live. Unfortunately, some of the methods that I thought were good actually damaged some of our property.

For example, we lost a hundred-foot oak tree due to a berm I unintentionally built over tree roots to stop flooding from a neighbor's yard. I had the best intentions, but it wasn't in harmony with the environment and killed the tree and our bank account.

The same thing can happen in our prayer lives. Even though we may be kind people with good intentions, we can contaminate the process and get off track. It's this interference or distortion of prayer that only leads to frustration, disappointment, pain, and depression.

The purpose of this chapter is to help you remove everything from your prayers that interferes with the true benefits of prayer—communion with God and power for living—supercharging. It's only when you recognize and remove these prayer contaminants that you have the best chance to know the deep peace, growth, and joyous service to others.

The only way to pray properly is to wholeheartedly accept the truths of The Universal Spiritual Way. You must be willing to reflect on what any group or person has told you about prayer. You must be willing to pray beyond a group's teachings and be completely transformed by God's spirit.

Avoiding Growth

People usually get off track with prayer because they don't get far enough beyond their basic human desires for an easy life, a quick fix, material things, predictability, power, and pleasure. Many also see prayer as a way to justify their conclusions and pride, and a way to simply get what they want in life.

Many people pray like a three-year-old. It's easy to revert to this primitive magical-thinking stage when the reality of adult responsibilities is in full force. And there are an endless number of prophets and programs promising a never-ending bonanza of self-gratification. In the end, it's an illusion and a diversion from the real joys and the true meaning of life.

> Prayer is not a substitute for work; it is a desperate effort to work further and to be efficient beyond the range of one's powers.
>
> —George Santayana, *Reason in Religion*

God placed all of us here so we would have a growth-stimulating, challenging environment to co-create resilient, persistent, courageous souls that will carry us on our eternal adventures. And, there is no greater joy than to grow closer to God in this faith adventure.

So, any kind of teaching or thinking that tries to deny or shortcut the challenges is delusional and misleading. Any prayer that we make asking to just be instantly transformed, to avoid challenges, goes nowhere. Any prayer asking for things to simply happen because we want them to, because we visualized them, is doomed to disappointment.

Prayers (and indeed all thinking) are based on basic assumptions and beliefs about ourselves, the universe, God, people, and the environment. If you have the wrong assumptions and beliefs, they'll lead to the wrong kinds of prayers. If you have a primitive view of God, you'll pray in a primitive way: You'll want God to be a cosmic Santa Claus. If you think the Universal Father is anything but perfect and kind, that he is like flawed human fathers, then you'll have a barrier to finding and loving Him.

If a person never gets beyond an ego-centered, self-centered drive, then all relations with God and others will only be seen as ways to satisfy base human drives and desires: pleasure, power, material things, and being told you're right and wonderful. Any prayer driven by any of those urges will never reach God and will bring no benefit to the person praying.

Here's what this could sound like:

Bad Prayer Example 1

God, I'm so sick of our nextdoor neighbors. They make so much noise and aren't friendly at all. When I ask them to move their cars out of my space, they just ignore me. I'm sick and tired of these people.

So I need your help. Please take them out of my life. I don't care how you do it, but my life would be so much better without them.

I've worked very hard to get the job I have and have a decent place to live, so please do this one thing for me. I can't stand this anymore! I deserve a pleasant place to live. I've had enough problems in my life and don't need any more.

The Father of the Universe appreciates your challenges and pain, but is focused on helping you grow, not making life easy. Our loving Divine Parent won't solve our problems but is with us through every one of them and cheering us on to stretch, to grow, to break out of our shells, again and again.

Prayer should never be used as a substitute for skill or knowledge. Again, God wants us to learn and know the joy of earning personal and intellectual growth. So, we shouldn't expect that if we pray for unearned knowledge or skill, that it will appear. Sure, we can pray for insights and revelations, but God wants us to make goals, gain skill and education, and achieve.

But, some people even go beyond those kinds of requests and expect God to change physical laws and work miracles. Of course, miracles do happen in the presence of great faith, but prayer should not be used as the default way to change the world or circumstances.

No wonder so many mistaught people grow so disappointed and depressed and eventually reject even the presence of God within. If a person persists in primitive ideas about God, they'll live in a world of superstition, ignorance, fundamentalism, and eventually, fanaticism.

The most liberating, most reliable beliefs about God incorporate the truth of the best philosophy and science, the beauty of the best art, and the goodness of all individual and collective acts of kindness and selflessness. It should be the main purpose of prayer to empower us to be conduits of this three-fold revelation of God.

So, let's all strive to leave behind stubbornness and crystallization of our thinking to accept the true realities and teachings from our Father within. It's only then that we'll be able to focus on and pray for growth as true spiritual adults and unite with our family around the world.

Have the courage to examine all the assumptions you've had about God and prayer, and let God teach you again. Give yourself permission to talk to God and live in the true light. Dedicate yourself to the thrilling adventure of mature, spiritual growth. Accept who our loving Father really is. Believe.

Prayer Today

We just saw how a focus on the wrong goals can lead to the wrong kinds of prayers and a lot of disappointment. There's actually another deeper level that separates us even further from God and spiritual growth: Many people don't know how to talk to God one-to-one or even don't pray to God at all.

> Prayer for many is like a foreign land. When we go there, we go as tourists. Like most tourists, we feel uncomfortable and out of place. Like most tourists, we therefore move on before too long and go somewhere else.
>
> —Robert McAfee Brown, *Prayer and Personal Religion*

Even though the majority of people in most cultures believe in some kind of God, their concepts of God are often barriers to knowing the real, loving, Divine Father. Century upon century of backward, negative, or superstitious beliefs about God have led not only to disappointment but to great separation and isolation from God for many people.

Millions upon millions of people actually pray to their unconscious minds and never really feel the surge of love and joy from direct contact with God. Many people are spiritual orphans who—while they pray—are simply reciting words and not connecting with God. God hears our sincere prayers and knows our thoughts, but it is only in true prayer that we begin to have contact with the Creator.

Good Prayer Example

God, it's been a real hard day at work. My team isn't getting the results I need, and I'm just not inspiring them. I've been doing a lot of thinking about this, and I think I need to be a better leader. I really need to grow up in many ways. That

> way, the team will have more confidence and be more effective.
>
> This has always been a big challenge for me. But, I also know that you can help me transform the way I work with this group. You can help me be more flexible, yet more confident.
>
> God, please give me the strength to make the kinds of changes I need to make. Please give me the insights and inner stability to be a better leader. I trust you completely and will listen to whatever you have to say. I will follow you and know you will give me exactly what I need. I am in your arms.

Many people die searching for the very source that lives within them. And they're usually thwarted by outdated, negative beliefs about God given to them by their parents, religious organizations, or other groups.

Some people find it virtually impossible to talk to God one-to-one because they believe they need a middleman or intermediary. They never get the amazing, endless stores of power and love from the inner-worship of God that comes after prayer. These people never get the depth of spiritual contact they deserve because they're gripped by the false teaching that God can only be known through a priest, teacher, or group.

Nothing is further from the truth. Nothing is more false. The loving, kind, sweet Universal Father lives in each of us and longs for direct contact. He longs for each of his countless children to discover their true nature and begin the joyous relationship and eternal adventure. His Spirit within is our direct contact with Him.

Many times, people pray only in the most challenging times—emergencies and crises. God always listens, but it's truly thoughtless and selfish to only pray to God when in need: This leads to very self-centered praying. Some people spend too much time praying for themselves and spend too much time praying in general, instead of doing things to help change their lives.

Here's what this kind of praying could sound like.

> **Bad Prayer Example 2**
> God, I want to change jobs. I don't like what I do and want something that I enjoy and where I make more money. I see so many other people with nice cars and houses and other things. I want this too. I deserve this, don't I? You're the most powerful Being in the universe, so please help me. Can't you see that I need some help? Aren't you willing to give me just a little bit more? I'm a good person. So, please help me. Bring abundance and power to my life. Bring prosperity so I can have a more comfortable life.

Prayer should never be a substitute for action. Prayer should be a stimulus to dynamic participation with God in transforming ourselves by serving, *really serving* others.

The Results of False Prayer

There can only be a few outcomes from persistent refusal to accept the light and continuing to ask God or the universe to make life easier or carry out our bidding: disappointment, frustration, depression, and sometimes, a descent into complete selfishness and darkness.

It's impossible for God to bring spiritual fruits or realities to a selfish person simply because the presence of so much selfishness blocks out God: Selfish thoughts close doors to God.

People can actually deceive themselves that they're following God, when they're actually following their own selfish desires or longstanding opinions. For example, I might think that stopping the construction of a senior center is in alignment with God's will. I put in a lot of extra volunteer hours and donate money to stop the center. I feel I'm helping God preserve a beautiful piece of land, or a quiet neighborhood. But, what's actually true is that I've been an environmental advocate all my life and am assuming that God supports my opinions.

Even if you perceive and follow the will of God, if you think you're making big sacrifices for God and focusing on this, you're actually reducing the effectiveness of your prayers. The consciousness of giving and the focus on personal sacrifice actually reduces the amount you're willing to give, as well as the effectiveness of your prayers. It's that element of self-focus that can be so damaging and is the age-old challenge for us to transcend; to get beyond the primitive drives of mere survival.

Selfish praying isn't ethical, and it goes against the divine justice of God. Asking for God to change events, to intervene, ultimately means that you're putting your needs above those of others. This is often hard to understand, especially watching the repeated spasms of genocide and recurring episodes of daily violence and destruction. We may think, "Why can't we just ask God to fix everything for us?" But, this is not ethical praying and lets us off the hook of giving and exerting, and transcending self.

Here's another unethical prayer:

Bad Prayer Example 3

God, I just learned today that they're opening a new business here in town. I've been out of work for a while, and I know a lot of other people are also trying to get jobs there. But, I *really* need this job.

So, you know I'm a good person. You know I'm generous. So, I'm asking for a little favor here: Please get me a job here. Please make the company pick me out of all the other people who are trying to get hired. I promise I'll pay you back and always remember what you did for me.

If we continually pray for only our benefit, if we keep praying against our enemies, if we only seek self-gain, we eventually lose the ability to see the light and make real spiritual choices. We eventually destroy ourselves.

In the end, prayer can be contaminated and warped by selfish desires and goals arising from our basic primitive survival urges. It's also often distorted by misleading teachings and outdated assumptions. Prayers can eventually be based on a fantasyland of selfishness, greed, and a lust for power.

As we saw in the last chapter, the best way to pray is to embrace the essential truth that you're a child of God and that others are your family, and that you can know this by faith: This is The Universal Spiritual Way. A life of eternal adventure and growth can be yours if you give all to God. And that starts with prayer and being willing to accept the answers and blessings that God provides.

> He who prays must commit himself and his wants to the transforming power of God. He must seek what is genuinely the greatest good and not merely the specific things which will satisfy his present wants.
>
> —Henry N. Wieman, *Normative Psychology of Religion*

So, use prayer to repeatedly fill your hunger for truth and desire for growth. Accept the divine reality within you with your God-given faith. Accept all that God is trying to give you: Expect and embrace the answers to your truest prayers. Come out of the darkness into the light of the Father of Light. Let your soul be energized with the greatest power of the universe that can completely transform you.

Spiritual Truths

Prayer is limited when it's based on primitive ideas of God and the universe.

Prayer becomes distorted when it's focused on satisfying primitive urges.

Prayers get off-track when they focus only on self.

Prayers that ask for God to do the work for us don't get the answers we envisioned.

Prayers for advantage or vengeance over others distort our spiritual selves.

Continued selfish, destructive praying eventually makes us unable to hear God.

What is the use of praying if at the very moment of prayer we have so little confidence in God that we are busy planning our own kind of answer to our prayer?

—Thomas Merton

Prayer Answers

The Divine Response

Chapter 6

There was a man I knew who was single; in fact, he was single most of his life and really longing for a woman to share his life with. He was a shy person with little self-confidence, who was more attractive and athletic than most. But, he just couldn't find the right person.

Since he believed in prayer, he prayed . . . and prayed . . . and prayed—for all of his adult life—for the woman of his dreams. He dated many women, but things never worked out.

Finally, he met one whom he thought was the right woman. He prayed and prayed that the relationship would work out, that she would fall in love with him as much as he was with her. But, she painfully ended the relationship and was soon dating a mutual friend, who was much more financially successful and confident.

My friend was utterly crushed and in the deepest depression of his life. Why couldn't God help him now? Why the excruciatingly painful wait?

But, that summer, he met the right person and became happily married. And . . . the woman he wanted to marry before?

. . . Well, she actually caused a lot of pain to every man she got involved with and gained quite a bad reputation.

In the end, my friend got the best answer to his prayers. He realized that God will give you everything you need, when you need it, in the way you need it, for as long as you need it. God meets our *true* needs and longs for us to embrace a full spiritual life of faith and joy.

We must remember that prayer is the most powerful tool to deal with any challenge, any pain. Prayer is the most effective way to get the power to continually see in new spiritual ways and to transform ourselves. Prayer leads to ultimate nourishment for the soul: worshipful communion with the Creator.

But, to achieve this kind of prayer, we need to change our beliefs about God and the purpose of life. We must be open-minded and refresh ourselves with the truths from God. We must be willing to let go of old beliefs and embrace the light of love—God's response.

Two Approaches to Life

The way we live is the direct result of what we believe. We can react as fearful animals or we can act as the children of God. Even a series of seemingly small beliefs add up to habits of thinking that lead to habits of living. Your conception of God, your beliefs about the purpose of life and the universe determine how you think and how you live.

Your beliefs can become barriers or pathways to God and truth. They can restrict the expression of your soul's true spiritual desires, or they can block progress to God and the reception of His love and truth. Your willingness to accept the truth and willingness to change is key.

Let's say that a person believes God is a stern, unforgiving judge, always looking for any flaws that He can punish: A person with this belief will think and live like their concept of God and adapt the way they relate to God as well. They're likely to be judgmental and critical, as well as continually afraid of doing wrong—of sinning. They'll see God as someone determining every life event and punishing every mistake.

They'll live in fear. And, ultimately, this fear is born from our evolutionary past in the old, primitive structures of our brains, not from the real God. They will have a religion of fear.

On the other hand, if people see God as a Divine Parent who loves us unconditionally, who wants us to realize our full potential and eternal destiny, then they'll feel tremendous peace, assurance, and security. They'll be inspired to become like God and help others do the same.

When you believe God is your Creator, provider, protector, and leader, there is no limit to your potential transformation. You will have a religion of love and service.

But, a person has to be willing to choose the light, to think about the good and the true, instead of thinking about fear, self-aggrandizement, power, and pleasure. What you think about, you'll eventually become or do, which will lead you to think those same seed thoughts again, even more intensely. The cycle is self-reinforcing; it perpetuates itself.

Following the light is the ultimate liberation of our minds to the path of discovery, joy, and service to others. It is the gateway to complete confidence and an endless reservoir of transformative power.

Without the burden of focusing on their own salvation, children of light are able to focus on a life of giving. When people realize that they can open the door to divine experience with faith—and faith alone–they're freed from complicated rules and rituals. When you accept the truths of The Universal Spiritual Way, you make possible the life God meant for you.

> Salvation is the gift of the Father and is revealed by his (Son). Acceptance by faith on your part makes you a partaker of the divine nature, a son or daughter of God. By faith you are justified; by faith you are saved; and by this same faith are you eternally advanced in the way of progressive and divine attainment.
>
> —Jesus, from *The Urantia Book*

You live with joy, power, and love. You'll transcend your evolutionary fear inheritance to know courage and triumph.

There are two ways to live: We can be slaves to the fear, laziness, selfishness, and material-focused survival instincts of our lower animal brains, or we can be the liberated faith - children of our Universal Father. It all depends on whether we're willing to accept the internal spiritual experiences that God endlessly provides to transform us, the FAITH he provides us.

Faith = Spiritual Experience. Belief=Acceptance of Faith—spiritual experience.

When you wholeheartedly accept the fact that you're a beloved child of the Creator of the universe, when you know that you have a direct line to God, you begin an endless adventure of true life. For, to be alive is to *know* you're alive. And to know you're alive means you know something of the real God.

When you pray as a faith-child of God, you already know that all your real needs will be met. You accept that God knows what's best and is giving you the incredible privilege of true life now and for eternity. And, because you'll be striving to become like God, you'll be praying for all that's needed to follow His guidance.

As we saw in Chapter 4, we should pray for growth. We should pray for courage, selflessness, spiritual-mindedness, motivation, and the ability to work hard to go the distance. Instead of asking God to do certain things, to change events, we seek to be one with the divine purpose in the roles that God wants us to play.

When we allow ourselves to accept the internal truths that God is broadcasting to us, then we have a real chance to transform our lives and our world into something profoundly beautiful, true, and good. The truths of The Universal Spiritual Way become the seeds for a beautiful spiritual garden, that is, if we only nurture them in prayer and inner-worship of God, and grow them with *action.*

If we pray in a primitive selfish way, then we'll expect God to answer our prayers with exactly what we're asking for: We're praying like very young children and not realizing the challenge and adventure of spiritual adulthood. To pray as an adult, means that you accept the responsibility to live your gifts for the most benefit to others and God.

The only way to truly live the ultimate spiritual life is to get the ultimate guidance—God's will. The Father of all will give you His opinion on all significant decisions in your life. He'll give you all the internal qualities and power you need to carry out your part of His masterful plan: your destiny path.

The Creator will always give you the best answers possible for whatever you're praying for. And, if you're focusing on doing

His will, then you'll be able to recognize and benefit from more and more of the answers that are coming from God.

The true benefit from prayer is that it energizes you so that you can transform yourself. It makes your old, animal mind flexible. It is the pathway to profound, immersive, sublime inner-worship of God. It enables your spirit within to begin to enlarge your soul and help you build up reserves of spiritual power for the adventure of following the Creator's guidance.

All personal transformation—answers—are possible, that is, if you pray and vigorously follow the divine leading within.

Unanswered Prayers

Everyone who prays and really pays attention, realizes that not all prayers are answered in the way they think they'll be answered: Our loving Father is going to do what's best for us. If we ask for something that's going to slow down or harm our spiritual growth, or distract us, then we can be sure that we're not going to get it. If we pray for things, not values, we won't get them.

Many times it may feel like God isn't interested, or is cruel, or may not exist. When we're faced with pain, sorrow, injustice, brutality, disease, and death, it can seem that God doesn't care or isn't even there. And when we pray for things, when we pray for certain outcomes, this seems especially true. When you believe in God and have the wrong expectations about God, the trials of life will only diminish your faith in the divine. The limitations of your concept of God will be even more eroded in the face of life's challenges and realities.

That's why it's so important to open your mind, to believe-accept, the true reality of God within. If we allow ourselves to suspend all preconceived notions and long-held opinions, then we can begin to improve our concepts of God. When we take down the barriers of rigid thinking and sit with the spirit of God within, we begin to be filled with faith and soon find that we have new understandings and notions of God that liberate us, even in the face of all life's challenges.

When you do this, you realize that your beliefs and understandings about God will continually evolve heavenward as God reveals more and more of himself and the truth about the universe. Our minds should be in a constant state of growth and renewal. The eternal truths of The Universal Spiritual Way will never change, but our understanding of them and the implications arising from them, will evolve upward as we become more spiritual, more mature, as we supercharge and grow our souls.

But this can only happen if we take the time to listen, to have a true conversation with God and immersive ourselves in communion with Him.

> Be not forgetful of prayer. Every time you pray, if your prayer is sincere, there will be new feeling and new meaning in it, which will give you fresh courage, and you will understand that prayer is an education.
>
> —Fyodor Dostoyesvsky

The more time we spend with God with open hearts and minds, the more we see of his endless loving nature and the purpose of life. We realize that the overarching will of the Father gives all of us a glorious role in the incredible adventure of life here and after death, in an endless universe. We realize that whatever our prayers are, God will meet our true needs.

Remember that whenever you pray, God is looking for ways to meet your underlying spiritual needs. And when he meets these, it can improve every aspect of your inner experience. The more you pray with openness and willingness, the more you are transformed.

When God answers our prayers, his matchless wisdom determines the right time, the right way, and the degree of the answer. We must remember that God—our Divine Parent—knows what's best for us, knows the most helpful response to our pleas.

Often, it would be a bad idea to give us what we're praying for. It may not seem like it in the moment, but when we look back with more mature eyes, often years later, we realize that getting what we wanted would've put us on the wrong path. If we pray out of selfishness, if we pray merely for self-gratification, pleasure, or power, God will challenge us to bear spiritual fruit instead.

When God doesn't answer our prayers in the way we think he should, it's often that he's delaying or modifying the answer for a later stage in our development. What sense does it make to answer even a spiritual plea when the answer can't be recognized or put to good use? God gives us what we need when we can handle it. God won't prematurely give us something we can't recognize or responsibly use.

It's important to realize that we're having a dialogue with God. Of course, it won't be as easy as having a conversation with another human person, but you'll begin to have insights and feel more and more love and guidance. Eventually, God's presence will be the most real experience in your life.

But this is only possible if you remove the barriers in your mind; you have to be willing to give up preconceived notions about God; you have to be willing to learn more about God and fill in your knowledge gaps; you have to be willing to give up superstitions that distort your understanding of the nature of God and the spiritual path. *You have to be willing to give up every intellectual assumption or priority that blocks knowing the ever-expanding, daily revelations of truth from God.*

Remember: Our thoughts, not our emotions and feelings lead us to God.

We have to realize that our thoughts and opinions can be wrong, but can always be improved. As we spend more and more time in prayer, as we spend more and more time serving others, we have to be willing to leave behind errors in our thinking and ideas about God.

There are many times that we don't even recognize answers from God because of our assumptions, as well as our ignorance and superstition. Once we realize the total peace, assurance, and security from God, we have the confidence to let God change our thoughts so we can change our living. When we're resting in our loving Father's arms, when we trust God completely, we can take the ultimate risk of changing ourselves.

He will always be there to catch us. He will always be there to comfort us. He will always be there to strengthen us for the rigors and joyous adventure of growth, of true life. When you believe this, you'll have the ultimate assurance and security to risk, fail, restart, reenergize, try again, stretch, discover, grow, and triumph to live your destiny— the life you were meant to live, the life that will give you real HAPPINESS.

If our prayers aren't answered in the way we think they should be answered, we have to realize that God is a spiritual being who will only give spiritual answers. He wants us to realize that the only things worth reaching for are eternal, infinite, and divine. Our role model should be God who is truth, beauty, and goodness, the source of love personified.

So when your prayer isn't answered yet, always remember that an answer is coming or is already here. Keep your eyes on the prize. God always answers prayers from people who really want to be better and do good. Focus on what is of *real* value. Strive for what will give *eternal* satisfaction. Live with *faith*. Liberate yourself from the cravings of the primitive animal brain to be lifted up in the light as an energized, *liberated* faith-child of the Creator.

Embrace every experience and influence of God as the answer to prayer.

Delayed Answers

We just saw that many times, even when it seems like God isn't answering our prayers, He really is. God gives us what we truly need to make the most spiritual progress and have the happiest, most joyful lives. But, we should also remember that God times the delivery of answers to our prayers to give us the most benefit.

Giving us answers to prayers at the wrong time can slow our progress and also make us confused and unhappy. Remember, God truly gives us what we need in the way we need it for as long as we need it, but at the right time—*when we need it*.

Of course, it's pretty hard to wait for an answer to prayer, especially when you have very strong yearnings and dissatisfactions. Let's face it, most people usually pray when they're in a crisis or have a pressing challenge or pain. So, it only makes sense that they want relief now. They want God to answer them *immediately*.

> The child is always within his rights when he presumes to petition the parent; and the parent is always within his parental obligations to the immature child when his superior wisdom dictates that the answer to the child's prayer be delayed, modified, segregated, transcended, or postponed to another stage of spiritual ascension.
>
> —*The Urantia Book*

But, our loving Father knows that there are many times when He can't answer our prayers immediately. If we really trust God, if we really understand the new truths that He is trying to reveal to us, we realize that He's going to do the best for us, that He's going to give us what we need when we need it for us to realize the most benefit and spiritual joy.

God also wants to make sure that the timing of the answer to your prayers best enables the incredible future He's reserved for you.

There's a unique destiny that you have; you're a unique person and God has a plan for your life to match your noble aspirations and gifts. His plan for your life fits into his master plan for the universe. The answers to your prayers are designed to help you best realize this glorious future.

Each of us is going to have a unique experience of God and a unique spiritual growth pattern. Each of us will have very specific needs based on who we are. You and I are both growing in the same direction toward God, but because you and I have different dispositions, gifts, experiences, and opportunities, our paths will be different.

Your personal unique spiritual evolution will determine when God can give you the answer to your prayers. Some answers can be given now and some need to await a time when you can recognize and benefit from them: Some answers can actually only be given after you die and are resurrected in the worlds to come.

We usually can't get instantaneous, comprehensive answers to our prayers. Yes, God gives us instantaneous strength and love, but his answers to our prayers must ultimately satisfy your soul's deepest spiritual needs and the longings underlying the prayers.

Whenever you express a sincere prayer from your very soul, God will only deny it if He has a better answer. If we keep in mind that we're children at the very beginning of an eternal adventure, and accept the fact that God is a perfect loving being, then we can trust that God will give us what we need, no matter what prayers we utter.

Patience is the key. If we remember that God placed us here to grow gradually, if we remember that we're part of the world governed by gradual change, then we realize that our spiritual lives are no different. All positive change requires focus, persistence, and regular, positive action.

> Never, in all your ascent to Paradise, will you gain anything by impatiently attempting to circumvent the established and divine plan by short cuts, personal inventions, or other devices for improving on the way of perfection, to perfection, and for eternal perfection.
>
> —*The Urantia Book*

Once we let go of our inborn impatience, we can begin to live in God's time. We can begin to know the total peace of life at his pace, following his way.

Prayer that Always Gets Answers

Whenever we pray, we must remember that the purpose of our lives should be to follow the divine will. The purpose of prayer is to help us transform ourselves so that we can better follow the plan of our Divine Father. And this path will lead to the ultimate, most beneficial, most joyful future possible for ourselves and others.

If you want to find ultimate happiness and satisfaction, if you want to find the most incredible joy and liberation possible in an unending future of discovery and success, then open yourself to the total change God wants to make in you, and be reborn each day. Pray profoundly.

You were meant to live an amazing, wonderful life, doing what gives you the most spiritual satisfaction. You were meant to find your life's work. You were meant to use your gifts for the ultimate good, healthy personal satisfactions, and the ultimate service to humankind. You were meant to discover that you are a child of the Creator, the One, The First Source and Center, The Universal Father.

The key for us is to be willing to continually try to wholeheartedly let go of everything and remove every barrier to hearing and following the will of God. *Prayer is the most effective fulcrum we can use.* Prayer helps us transform our thinking from the inside out to nourish and grow our souls to dynamic action.

Gradually, if we're committed to perceiving and following the way of the Creator, that way will become clearer and clearer. When we bring every decision before God, when we try to listen without interference, we gradually hear more and more. We gradually receive God's assurance that we truly know what he wants us to do.

And since we realize that doing the Father's will is the secret to a better life, our prayers soon ask for help in knowing and doing that divine will.

When you pray to God for inner strength or for the benefit of the spiritual growth of others, and if God supports this desire, then *it will come to pass*, sooner or later. When you work in partnership with God to manifest his desires, when it is your will that the Father's will is done, then that inner blessing or project succeeds.

When your prayer is motivated by spiritual longing and love, when it comes from the deepest place in your soul, it's answered. So, when you pray, pray from your soul; speak words of inner spiritual longing and true desire for growth and service to others.

Remember that no prayer is answered unless born of this true soul longing and nurtured by your faith, your acceptance, of the true reality of God within you. When you make time for God and allow yourself to be immersed in the light of His love, then you can truly pray from your soul and trust God to give you the full answer to your deepest, spiritual longings.

Only then can you be supercharged.

We need to think about prayer in a completely new way: The purpose of prayer is not to change God, but to change ourselves. The purpose of prayer is not to satisfy the primitive desires of our lower brains but to amplify and experience and fulfill the desires of our spiritual selves—our souls—to become our better future selves revealed by the spirit within.

When we change our prayer-motivation, we allow ourselves to totally surrender to the will of the Universal Father. We might be tempted to think that we become puppets with no real choice. But, we're actually amplifying our own free will and experiencing more of real life. We experience more and more moments where we know that we know, where we know God and our true selves—our souls.

> It is astonishing how the act of placing our own will as far as possible in unison with the Will of God restores our tranquility.
>
> —Arthur Christopher Benson

And this total surrender to God, this total trust that God will answer all our prayers in the best possible way, leads to the best possible life. When we cooperate with God and accept what he wants to give us, we take part in a beautiful alchemy of ourselves that leads to everything that's good in a person, and ultimately to everything that is good in the world.

The truest answer to prayer is peace, assurance, security, and the power to enable total transformation. The truest answer to prayer is the supercharging of your soul. The truest answer to prayer is the invitation and nourishment for more life, the endless life of a child of the Creator of the universe.

Spiritual Truths

The way we pray and live is determined by our beliefs.

There are only two ways to live: animal or spiritual.

The only way to live the ideal, spiritual life is to follow the will of God.

God always gives you the best answers possible to your prayers.

God often does not give you the answers you want, or provides answers later than you wanted them.

When you pray to know the will of the Father and for spiritual growth, you will always welcome God's answers.

Prayer is the most perfect and most divine action that a rational soul is capable of. It is of all actions and duties the most indispensably necessary.

—Augustine Baker

Prayer in Action

Examples of Faith

Chapter 7

We've learned a lot about prayer so far, but nothing can take the place of good examples from those on the path to God. This chapter is a collection of prayers I found in books and on the Internet. I hope you find joy and inspiration to grow your prayer life into a fountain of life-sustaining peace, assurance, security, strength, confidence, courage, power, and selflessness.

Father God, there are so many decisions to make and I don't seem to know what is the best for now or for the future. You said if we lack wisdom, all we need to do is ask you. I really need you to pour wisdom into my mind today. Thank you!

—Anonymous

Lord, make me happy with Awareness of Thee. Give me freedom from all earthly desires, and above all, give me Thy joy that outlasts all the happy and sad experiences of life.

—Paramahansa Yogananda

God of our ancestors in faith, by the covenant made on Mount Sinai. You taught Your people to strengthen the bonds of family through faith, honor, and love. Look kindly upon my friend, a mother who sought to bind her children to You. Bring her to Your heavenly home where the saints dwell in blessedness and peace.
Amen.

—Anonymous

O Allah, remove from my heart the love of
everything not beloved to You.

—Anonymous

Let us be at peace, let people's souls be relaxed...
Remove all evil from our path.

—Nuer/Sudan prayer

Holy God, your knowledge of me exceeds what I grasp or see in any moment; you know me better than I know myself. Now, help me to trust in your mercy, to see myself in the light of your holiness, and grant me the grace that I may have true contrition, make an honest confession, and find in you forgiveness and perfect remission. Amen.

—Saint Augustine

Glorious Father and Mother, in one parent combined,
Loyal would we be to your divine nature.

Your own self to live again in and through us
By the gift and bestowal of your divine spirit,

Thus reproducing you imperfectly in this sphere
As you are perfectly and majestically shown on high.

Give us day by day your sweet ministry of brotherhood
And lead us moment by moment in the pathway of loving service.

Be you ever and unfailingly patient with us
Even as we show forth your patience to our children.

Give us the divine wisdom that does all things well
And the infinite love that is gracious to every creature.

Bestow upon us your patience and loving-kindness
That our charity may enfold the weak of the realm.

And when our career is finished, make it an honor to your name,
A pleasure to your good spirit, and a satisfaction to our soul helpers.

Not as we wish, our loving Father, but as you desire the eternal good
of your mortal children,

Even so may it be.

—*The Urantia Book*

Blessed are You, LORD our God, King of the universe, Who has kept us alive, sustained us, and enabled us to reach this season.

—*The Torah*

Oh Lord, kindly forgive my wrong actions done knowingly or unknowingly, either through my organs of action or through organs of perception or by my mind. Glory unto Thee oh Lord, who is the ocean of kindness.

—Anonymous

[I ask] God to fill you with the knowledge of his will in all spiritual wisdom and understanding, so that you may live worthily of the Lord and please him in all respects—bearing fruit in every good deed, growing in the knowledge of God, being strengthened with all power according to his glorious might for the display of all patience and steadfastness, joyfully giving thanks to the Father who has qualified you to share in the saints' inheritance in the light.

—Saint Paul

O Allah, give me patience when things don't go my way. You know what is best for me, so help me accept what You have decreed for me and make me among Your grateful servants. Amen.

—Anonymous

Master of the universe, Supreme, effulgent Being!

The false gods rule our lives and our troubled minds,

And drive us into the midst of deluding whirlpools.

Give me the wisdom to discern the path hidden from us,

By which your dearest devotees always reach you.

—Jayaram V

Creator of all we are! All we have! All we ever shall be!

I give to You my most humble gratitude.

I thank You for life and all that pertains to life about me.

I thank You for giving me this opportunity of life in this form so that I may walk among Your wonders with knowledge and be given the option to be considerate and to care.

I give You gratitude for those untold billions of lives that graciously gave themselves over to maintain this life over these many years, humbling me by their unselfish sacrifice just to keep me walking here. So much so as to realize the sacredness of life, upon this earth I share. Doubly grateful with each day, just knowing You placed them there.

I ask Your forgiveness Oh Great MYSTERY for all the petty things I've done. Cursing, griping and groaning over pains and shames that's done, with so little consideration for all the wisdom won.

With gratitude for all that was given and all that may yet to come. I give myself unto Your keeping to let Your will be done. Humbly asking and beseeching to use this aged parchment to face Your drum. Stretch it to its limit until under Your slightest touch it gives its loudest strum. Your drum signals given to all about and all that's yet to come.

Forgive me if I sound selfish Oh Mystery after all you have already done. But for myself I have but one wish, perhaps a foolish one. That on that day when the mystery unfolds before me, when the work of this flesh is done, That I may utter with my final breath, "I DID ALL I SHOULD HAVE DONE!"

Thus I pause in this unending prayer, ending as was begun, with undying gratitude for everything You have given and for all that You have done.

—Wanish, Blue Turtle

O Allah! Enlighten what is dark in me. Strengthen what is weak in me. Mend what is broken in me. Bind what is bruised in me. Heal what is sick in me. Straighten what is crooked in me. Revive whatever peace and love died in me.

—Anonymous

Lord, make me an instrument of your peace,
Where there is hatred, let me sow love;
Where there is injury, pardon;
Where there is doubt, faith;
Where there is despair, hope;
Where there is darkness, light;
Where there is sadness, joy;

O Divine Master,
Grant that I may not so much seek
To be consoled as to console;
To be understood as to understand;
To be loved as to love.

For it is in giving that we receive;
It is in pardoning that we are pardoned;
And it is in dying that we are born to
eternal life.

—St. Francis

My God, the soul You have given me is pure. You created it, You formed it, and You breathed it into me, and You guard it while it is within me, and one day You will take it from me, and restore it to me in the time to come. As long as the soul is within me, I will thank You, HaShem my God and God of my ancestors, Master of all works, Lord of all souls. Blessed are You, LORD, who restores souls to lifeless bodies.

—*The Torah*

Oh, Great Spirit, whose voice I hear in the wind,
Whose breath gives life to all the world.

Hear me; I need your strength and wisdom.
Let me walk in beauty, and make my eyes ever behold
the red and purple sunset.

Make my hands respect the things you have made and
my ears sharp to hear your voice

Make me wise so that I may understand the things
you have taught my people. Help me to remain calm and
strong in the face of all that comes towards me. Let me
learn the lessons you have hidden in every leaf and rock.

Help me seek pure thoughts and act with the intention
of helping others. Help me find compassion without
empathy overwhelming me.

I seek strength, not to be greater than my brother,
but to fight my greatest enemy - Myself.

Make me always ready to come to you with clean
hands and straight eyes. So when life fades, as the
fading sunset,
my spirit may come to you without shame.

—Anonymous

Our Father who is in heaven,
Hallowed by your name.

Your kingdom come; your will be done
On earth as it is in heaven.

Give us this day our bread for tomorrow;
Refresh our souls with the water of life.

And forgive us every one our debts
As we also have forgiven our debtors.

Save us in temptation, deliver us from evil,
And increasingly make us perfect like yourself.

—Jesus, from *The Urantia Book*

Part III

Unlimited Transformation

Of all spiritual disciplines prayer is the most central because it ushers us into perpetual communion with the Father.

—Richard C. Foster

A Prayer Jump-Start

Steps to Sing to God

Chapter 8

Success in any activity or area in life depends on following the right steps in the right way, with the right technique. Just think about rock climbers for a minute. Everything they do before and during the climb contributes or detracts from their goal of reaching the summit and having a great experience.

First, they need to scout out a rock to climb, whether it's standing straight up, or it's embedded in the side of a hill. After this, they'll want to do some research by talking to friends, reading books, or watching videos about the place they want to go. Next, they'll want to think about their own abilities, as well as those of their partners for the climb.

Since they've done their research, they'll arrive at the rock with all the equipment they need. Then it all depends on concentration, judgment, and technique.

At the bottom of the cliff, they'll begin by sorting out their equipment and then putting on their safety harnesses. They'll unpack their ropes and then carefully use the proper knot to tie themselves to the rope. They'll then strap their equipment across their shoulders, take the rope, and begin to place their hands and feet on the rock and carefully move upward.

Prayer, like rock climbing, has a set of steps and techniques that leads to success. Although you can make progress with a good heart and faith, you'll make much more progress with the right steps.

Of course, you can pray to or worship God anywhere, at any time, without going through the steps I'll outline. And, depending on your state of spiritual health, you may already be carrying out an ideal spiritual practice unconsciously. But, you probably won't reach profound states of God consciousness and soul nourishment without the process I'll discuss. Like all things in life, complete focus—wholehearted attention and effort—brings the best outcomes, real progress.

As you've seen, profound prayer is the most effective way to supercharge your soul with the life of the spirit-energy from God. Whatever personal quality you're missing, be it motivation, strength, faith, courage, or altruism, you'll receive everything you can handle when you come with sincerity in prayer to God.

This chapter will show you the essential ingredients for success and the techniques to deepen your experience and accelerate your growth.

The Foundation of Success

The first thing to remember is that any effort you make with a sincere desire to know God and grow will give you progress. It may be slow at first, but, as you make more time for God and improve your divine conversation, you'll move more quickly.

Please remember that the most important thing is that you're growing, you're moving forward. Again, you need to accept the fact that you live in an evolutionary world, which means that you must follow a gradual path to evolve yourself to a new self. It's true that there is a moment when you accept the truths of The Universal Spiritual Way and know God and are reborn. But, everything after is likely to be a slow, gradual process of spiritual transformation.

The most important ingredient you can bring is your attitude. You need to be not just positive, but you need to come to prayer willing to do what is necessary to grow, willing to change your beliefs and behaviors, willing to spend time with God and to serve others. So, come with the open, trusting, enthusiastic, vibrant heart of a child into the arms of your loving Divine Parent.

Whatever challenge you face, whatever weakness you must overcome, your attitude is the gateway for being able to accept everything that God is trying to give you NOW. Everything you do in your spiritual life depends on your fundamental response to who you are, to God, and to the outer world of people and things.

> I am still determined to be cheerful and happy, in whatever situation I may be; for I have also learned from experience that the greater part of our happiness or misery depends upon our dispositions, and not upon our circumstances.
>
> —Martha Washington

Building on your attitude are the beliefs that your attitude fosters. And, the most powerful beliefs are those of The Universal Spiritual Way: You're a child of a perfect divine parent, all are your family, and you can have an endless life of peace, challenge, adventure, and joy if you use your faith and follow God's will. You are a child of a loving Divine Father.

The second most important tool is your thoughts. When you allow God to spiritualize your thinking, you'll gradually see negative thinking transform into true, beautiful, good, confident, and courageous thoughts. Your mind is a critical tool for your prayer life because you use it to respond to God and apply prayer techniques.

When and Where to Pray

Make no mistake: You can pray anywhere and at any time. If you're sincere, if you use the foundations of prayer, you'll find some level of nourishment from God. But, just like a garden, your mind, body, and soul should be cared for. If you regularly tend and condition the soil, if you remove the weeds, if you give it light and water, you'll see it flourish.

There is a misconception about prayer: Some believe that to be more spiritual means that you're less organized and deliberate, but any artist can tell you that progress depends on deliberately creating the conditions for growth and following sustaining habits.

Don't be afraid to schedule time to pray. Don't be afraid to remove other things from your calendar to make time for God. You should schedule time for God each morning and evening. Start out with just a few minutes, and don't try to do too much at once. Just make sure that every day you're sticking to your schedule and praying, even for just a short time.

> The more complex society becomes, and the more the lures of civilization multiply, the more urgent will become the necessity for God-knowing individuals to form such

protective habitual practices designed to conserve and augment their spiritual energies.

—*The Urantia Book*

Soon, you'll discover that it's just a little bit easier each day to stay on your prayer schedule. As you spend more time with God, as you open your heart to the divine presence, the spirit of the Father within you will change your thoughts and invigorate you with hope and power: It will be easier and easier to stay on the path since you're being nourished and thinking more spiritual thoughts.

And, almost surprisingly, you'll find that you'll be spontaneously praying at other times of the day. In fact, the deepening of the connection that you grow in scheduled prayer increases the amount of time you spontaneously pray. Gradually, the consciousness of God that you initiate in the morning will extend more and more throughout your day until you finally pray before you sleep.

The ideal life is one where we're conscious of God constantly and pray to Him quite frequently.

Next, we have to think about the places where we actually pray. Sure, we need to be sincere and earnest and try hard. But, if we don't have the right place to pray, it will be more difficult to get started and reach the level of contact with our God that we crave and need so badly.

The ideal place to pray is in nature, but, most of us will end up praying regularly at home, inside a house or building. I encourage you to create an environment for prayer as best you can that meets these criteria:

- **Privacy.** You're alone. This location is a private area where you can pray for significant amounts of time without someone being in the room. It is not a public or group space. No one can see you when you're praying.
- **Quiet.** This place doesn't have any conversations or voices or sounds that you find disturbing. Everyone has a different tolerance level, but, if you're trying to listen to the Divine, any level or frequency of disturbing noise can disrupt you, especially if it occurs randomly.
- **Comfort.** At first, this isn't as big a factor. But, as you begin to spend more and more time with God, you'll be distracted if you're uncomfortable. This varies from person to person, especially for those with physical challenges. Just make sure that you're comfortable, but not so comfortable that you fall asleep. Keeping your back vertical, if possible, is a great technique.
- **Beauty.** The ideal place to pray is outside in an inspiring place, but, most of us will be praying inside. So, try to make your room more beautiful, or, if you can, reserve a room for your praying. Hang pictures of nature or beautiful art or architecture.

And so, when you begin to regularly pray in a good location, when you pray randomly at other times of the day, you'll find yourself communing with the Father's spirit within you. You'll begin to feel God more and be one with God in the important decisions of your life.

Spirituality won't just be one corner of your life, but the essence of your life. Everything you think will be changed by the gentle leading of the Father's spirit, followed by your attitude, and realized in your actions. Prayer is the breath of the soul and will be the way to continual nourishment for your life.

The Prayer and Growth Cycle

The essence of prayer is asking for help from God to transform yourself. When you have a challenge, problem, need, or worthy goal or desire, you should share it with God. Ask for the power and transformation from the Father's spirit within to realize a better future for yourself and others.

Never forget, the focus of true spirituality is not gains for the self, but growth and joy for others. If we believe in a perfect, loving Universal Father, we're assured that all our true needs are met, and we have an eternal existence as long as we try to follow the divine leading. Our loving parent will give us everything we need, when we need it, in the way we need it, for as long as we need it to help us transform ourselves to meet any challenge.

When you're assured that God helps you even before you ask for help, you have the peace and confidence to focus on others. You can assume that if you follow the leading of God, your salvation is assured and all your true needs are met. You're released for the joyful, self-forgetful service of a liberated son or daughter of the Divine Father.

But, none of this personal transformation, none of the benefits of prayer, are possible without us doing something for ourselves or others. Action in the real world enlarges our capacity to benefit from conversation and communion with our Eternal Father.

> When man consecrates his will to the doing of the Father's will, when man gives God all that he has, then does God make that man more than he is.
>
> —*The Urantia Book*

So, before we even begin to pray, we should be doing all we can to meet the challenge, the need, the desire, or the goal. God won't do anything for us that we cannot do ourselves. It's not that he's stingy or stern, but that He knows the most effective way for us to grow is to put out effort. And, our efforts enlarge our capacity to handle more divine power.

Again, before we ask for something from God, we should be doing *everything* we possibly can to transform ourselves and achieve our worthy life goals and service for others.

It's important to realize that prayer is only the beginning of an incredible, potentially never-ending inner experience with God. After we pray, we should tell God everything that we're thankful for; we should completely empty our hearts of every bit of appreciation and adoration we have for God. We should follow prayer with happy memories of the gifts of God and consciousness of true blessings. And this thankfulness should give way to complete and profound expression of our adoration, our inner-worship of God.

When we allow prayer to transport us to thanksgiving and worshipful communion with the very Creator of the universe, we feel indescribable peace, joy, and confidence, and have the vision to go out and act with greatness. True ethical praying is the ultimate stimulus for self-forgetful service and resulting personal transformation.

We are completely nourished—supercharged.

Prayer, thankfulness, worship, communion with God, and action, are the secrets of spiritual success in this life and in the eternal future. True religion is a way of living with God and others to forget our animal ego selves and liberate to become our true spiritual selves. Each day we wake up to who we really are—and are becoming—as children of God.

The Prayer Process

Once you've found a reliable place to pray and scheduled the time, it's important to follow the process of prayer. But, you don't need to be expert in prayer, or even the prayer process, to see benefits. Any time that you sincerely express to God your desire for truth and growth and service to others, you'll get divine blessings; you'll get an answer to your prayers.

But, just like in our rock climbing example, you're going to see the most benefit, the most progress, if you learn the art of divine conversation. Prayer is just that—a relationship, a friendship with God.

When it's time for your scheduled prayer, the first thing you need to do is immediately go to your place of prayer: Don't think about anything else; don't try to do one more thing; don't let anything distract you from beginning your prayer session. *It's absolutely critical that you stop doing other things*, that you eliminate anything that would compete with your time for prayer.

Of course, all of us have obligations to our physical and mental health, our spouses and partners, children, family, friends, work, and society. But, our highest obligation is to God and our spiritual growth. Even though we have a lot to juggle, it's possible to make time and find a place for prayer: God will help you do this if you're willing to sometimes let go of time you spend on other things.

> A simple life is not seeing how little we can get by with—that's poverty—but how efficiently we can put first things first . . . When you're clear about your purpose and your priorities, you can painlessly discard whatever does not support these, whether it's clutter in your cabinets or commitments on your calendar.
>
> —Victoria Moran

So, when it's time for prayer, stop everything you're doing and think only of going to your place to pray. Let those around you know that this is your private time, and you shouldn't be disturbed. If you state this plainly and respectfully and begin to show this habit in your life, most others will respect you. If this doesn't work, you'll need to find a way to be alone in your private place.

First, take these steps in order, and then repeat any of them as needed to get to a profound level of prayer:

1. **Go to your space and take your position.** If you can, close the door in your room of prayer. Sit or kneel with your back vertical, your head forward, with relaxed arms and hands. If you have a physical challenge, just find the best position where you can stay the most alert for a sustained period.

2. **Relax and meditate.** A relaxed, clear mind is the foundation of prayer. So, as you're sitting or kneeling, take deep breaths and exhale slowly. Ask God's spirit within to help you clear your mind and open your heart.

At first, you probably won't be very effective in this meditation, but you will begin to make good progress.

Make sure not to look for perfection here. In the very beginning, you may only be able to calm down a little. But, as you do this more often, you'll get better at it. *Any effort you make here will help your praying experience.*

3. **Be wholehearted.** Once you've calmed and cleared your mind, you can express your innermost longings and feelings. When you're still, you're much more able to give everything to the moment. So when you pray, do just that. Remember to put your whole heart into it, even if from time to time you get distracted or tired. Put all your energies into expressing yourself to the very depths of your being, and then completely open up to the divine embrace. *Being wholehearted is the key to prayer.*

4. **Express your faith and hunger for growth.** As you sit there with God, accept the experience you're having and will continue to have. When you experience the presence of God, when you feel the Divine Father's total love, when you begin to have new insights, when you feel all the blessings of that experience begin to emerge in the very moment of prayer, accept what you're experiencing. BELIEVE.

   This is often the most difficult part of beginning your spiritual path. Many of us have been trained to only believe what our societies, religions, groups, or others tell us is true. All too many people will try to rob you of your spiritual experience. When you're in prayer and these doubts, disbeliefs, and prejudices come into your mind, don't look at them and dwell on them: They are meaningless vapors that will evaporate in the clear atmosphere of divine truth.

Clear your mind and let the truth from God's spirit within shine to change your thoughts. When you begin to perceive a feeling or thought that is different from your assumptions and beliefs, pay attention to it rather than your old ways of thinking. If you focus on your old thoughts, they will crowd out the new spiritual thoughts. *Make the effort to keep focusing on the new spiritual thoughts*, and they will reveal a clearer reality, today, and every day, for eternity.

Don't be afraid. God will be with you every step of the way. He'll give you the confidence and the strength to banish fear with courage, and the total joy of knowing the real truth about Him. Always remember: *The best place to find the truth is within your very self.* The spirit of the Universal Father lives within you and will give you a profound assurance and life direction if you only let go of prejudices and preconceived notions about Him and the spiritual life.

As you accept—believe—what you're experiencing, also remind yourself of and celebrate the truths of The Universal Spiritual Way. Affirm with God that you accept the fundamental truths He gives you, and welcome the adventure of endless discovery of new and expanded truths and a life of matchless service.

5. **Pour out your heart.** Building on your wholeheartedness, as intensely and deeply as you can, tell God everything that is on your mind: thoughts, emotions, desires, goals, problems, fears, dreams, anything that is concerning or enticing you.

   I can't emphasize this enough: *Use total intensity and depth in sharing your thoughts and feelings with God.* This will allow you to move into true prayer and be open to the leading and inspiration of God.

   Always listen longer than you speak. The whole point of prayer is to get divine guidance and power. So, like any good conversation, you need to let the other person speak. You can't hear anything, can't really listen, until you stop talking, until you stop expressing. And this goes for the entire prayer process.

   Have your say, but then listen to God.

6. **Ask God for help.** This is really part of Step Five, but ask God for help. Ask our kind Divine Parent for help for yourself and others, your family and friends. Share the situation that you and others are facing, and ask God to give the spiritual transformation to meet a challenge, to increase hope, to bring peace and spiritual healing, to bring power.

   And if you have any doubts about what to pray for, just tell God about these doubts and send out your prayers. He'll give you what you need with the best answers possible.

If you're trying to decide what to do, ask God for help. God won't do your thinking or homework for you, but He will give you the guidance you're capable of receiving based on the thinking and homework that you did. When you face a challenge, think about it deeply and try to outline what to do. Of course, if you have no idea what to do, God will help you.

Share with God your thoughts on the problem and what you think should be done. Give God the reasons for your conclusions, and tell Him where you're stuck. It may be that you just can't figure out what to do, or you have no idea how you're going to get what you need. Remember, God is not a Santa Claus giving us whatever we ask for, but He is our loving parent who will give us what we need to transform ourselves to live under any circumstances to meet our true spiritual needs.

7. **Pray for guidance and listen.** When you're just not sure what to do, ask God for His advice. When you pray for God's guidance with all your heart, it means that you've opened your heart and mind to whatever He has to say to you. It means that you have the peace, assurance, and security to let go of your opinions and take hold of His hand.

   This doesn't mean that you're going to instantly get the answers you need, but it does mean that you'll make progress in getting to those answers. Every sincere effort you make to pray for wisdom and guidance from God gets you closer to that wisdom and guidance. Like cleaning a dirty window, our wholeheartedness will begin to let in the true light of truth and the *specific guidance* the Father has for your life.

This may take days or weeks or months, but you'll know when you have the answers. The key is to be patient and wait until you reach that point of assurance and confidence of the guidance from God, and feel His love. Don't assume that what you think is the guidance of God is completely accurate the first time you ask. Go back to God *again and again* and *again* in prayer until you're absolutely certain.

8. **Tell God what you're thankful for and worship.** By now you've talked, listened, and talked, again and again, as much as needed. This may be a short or long time, and can vary from prayer session to prayer session. But, once you've made your requests to God, it's time to tell God what you're thankful for.

   No matter what circumstances you face, find something you're thankful for. Honestly open your mind, and share everything with your complete heart. Realize the incredible miracle of even being self-conscious, of seeing the world, of knowing others, of knowing the very Creator of the universe.

   Express your adoration and appreciation for God. Tell Him everything you adore about Him. Acknowledge every wonderful experience you've had of Him and all that He's done for you. Worship the Father of lights. Lose yourself in the sea of divine love as you share your love for God.

This worship is the pinnacle of the inner experience, with prayer as the doorway. *It's here that you gain the most power and build reserves for inner transformation.* Inner-worship of God is the greatest experience and the greatest source of life. It's here that we truly know ourselves and God.

9. **Act on God's guidance.** This isn't part of prayer, but is the prelude to more effective prayer. Even though you may pray a lot and receive spiritual nourishment, unless you follow God's guidance and get out into the real world and help others, you'll be stuck. Unless you act on what you're given within, you'll never progress and will eventually lose faith and become depressed.

The Prayer Process of Eternal Life

The prayer process is a cycle of life, and ultimately, eternal life. You should always begin and return to prayer. Here, you'll be nourished, energized, and supercharged for growth, service to others, greatness, and triumph. Here, you are **remade** as you give all to God. Here, you cooperate with God to transform yourself into an eternal, faith-child of God.

Here, the impossible growth becomes possible—the norm.

Again, just visualizing what you want does not make it happen. There is no substitute for real action. You need to put out consistent, courageous, selfless effort. But, when you act, you become more and more liberated for life—a real life of unimagined spiritual joy and accomplishment. You'll become part of the spiritual workers for God. You'll be a triumphant child of light.

Take a minute to review the Prayer Process of Eternal Life on the next page. This will help you make great strides in developing essential spiritual habits to supercharge your soul. Eventually, you'll develop your own set of healthy spiritual habits based on the truths and principles of prayer and inner-worship of God.

At first it will take a lot of effort to start moving. But, once you are in some kind of motion, it will get easier and easier to continue this process. Remember to start out very slowly, be consistent each day, and gradually increase as God leads you to a deeper relationship with Him and a fuller outer life.

Inner needs should lead us to seek inner nourishment. Once filled, we should be grateful and want to share with others. The spiritual exercise of serving others will lead to deeper desires to spend time with God and eventually, back to and even richer life of joy, love, and service: true happiness.

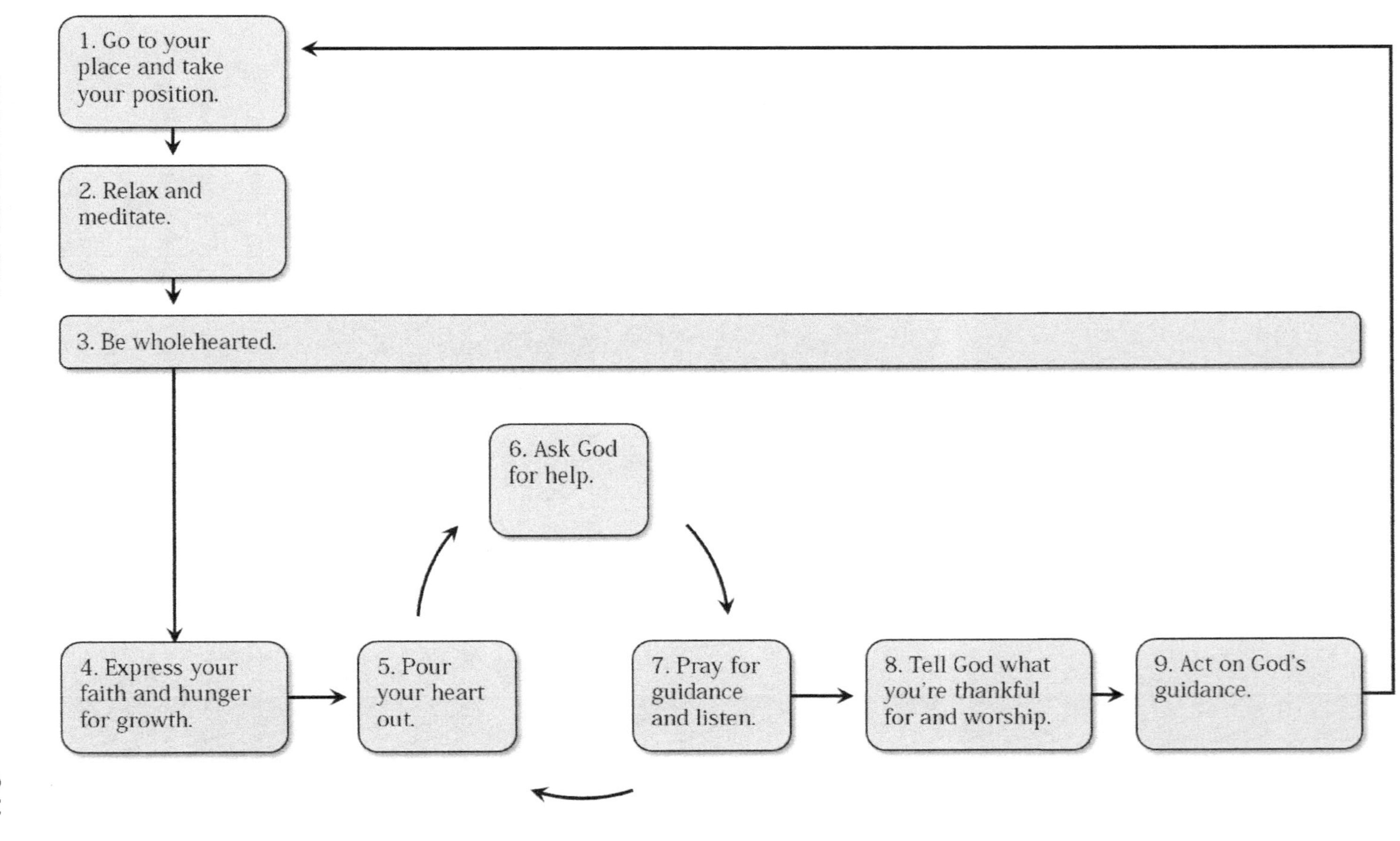

The Prayer Process of Eternal Life

Making Plans for Profound Prayer

Now it's time to put what you know about prayer into action. You might want to create a prayer journal and reflect on the questions below. I've also provided a checklist to help you prepare for prayer. Of course, you can remove or add to these in your journal. This is just a starting point:

- What are your biggest life challenges and goals?
- How do you hope prayer will help you?
- How do you need to change your understanding of God, what life is for, and what you're thankful for?
- What beliefs, misconceptions, prejudices, and habits are limiting your growth?
- When and where do you pray?
- How can you improve your prayer process?
- What obstacles or other priorities do you need to remove to make a place for prayer?
- Who can support you in getting better at prayer?

Here are a couple of tools you can use to establish and improve your prayer life.

A Prayer Plan Checklist	
	Find a quality place and prepare it.
	Schedule time to sit and think about your challenges and beliefs.
	Set two times a day to pray for at least five minutes each.
	Adjust or eliminate other activities.
	Share your prayer journey with others who pray regularly.
	Create a firm foundation of physical and mental health; be sure to socialize.
	Serve others in your routine activities and schedule times for more service.

The Prayer Process
1. Go to your space and take your position.
2. Relax and meditate.
3. Be wholehearted.
4. Express your faith and hunger for growth.
5. Pour out your heart.
6. Ask God for help.
7. Pray for guidance and listen.
8. Tell God what you're thankful for and worship.
9. Act on God's guidance.

All this talk and turmoil and noise and movement
is outside the veil;
inside the veil is silence and calm and peace.

—Bāyazīd Bisṭāmī

Always remember that God has given you the garden of your mind and soul to nurture. This is the most precious gift you have. Be sure to nurture it each day, keep it free of pests and poisons, and feed it with the light of life.

Anything that you'll achieve in this world requires that you maintain a clear vision of your goal, create a plan, gain strength and power, and put your plan into action. The most important project, the greatest mission of your life, is to live your destiny as a daughter or son of the Divine Father.

And the most effective way to keep your garden healthy and expanding is to consistently devote yourself each day to periods of quality prayer. Whatever challenge you face, whatever power you need, whatever answers you seek, God will provide.

It all starts with prayer.

Spiritual Truths

Success in prayer depends on focus, regular frequency, commitment, and technique.

An attitude of spiritual growth and belief in the truths of The Universal Spiritual Way is the most important prayer foundation.

You should make regular time for prayer in a conducive environment.

First comes prayer, then thanksgiving and inner-worship with God, then action/spiritual exercise, and then back to the nourishment of prayer and worship.

Optimal prayer depends on proper preparation and a series of key steps.

The most effective way to improve your spiritual growth is to pray.

Be not constantly overanxious about your common needs. Be not apprehensive concerning the problems of your earthly existence, but in all these things by prayer and supplication, with the spirit of sincere thanksgiving, let your needs be spread out before your Father who is in heaven.

—Jesus, from *The Urantia Book*

Ideal Prayer

Achieving the Infinite

Chapter 9

Our lives are miracles. We start out as two cells that join to become the blueprint of a unique individual. In less than a year, we're ready to emerge into an outer world of endless sensations, people, and possibilities.

At first, we can't really do much more than eat, sleep, pee, poop, breathe, and cry. But, pretty quickly, we begin to perceive others and instinctively use sounds to get our needs meet. We speak, and in a relatively short time, begin building relationships.

In time, we can crawl, and then soon, walk. We learn about food, people, animals, nature, clothing, danger, and pleasure. Within a short time, we're interacting with other children and eventually start school. Gradually, our progress becomes less automatic and then completely dependent on our efforts.

Within a few years, we leave school and launch ourselves into our lives, hopefully, to follow our dreams and add as much truth, beauty, and goodness to this world as we can.

While this journey from two joined cells to a unique adult individual is nothing short of miraculous, our spiritual transformations can be even more amazing. But, unlike the basic physical and mental changes, we must rely on prayer to supercharge our souls to inspire our minds to reach out and touch the infinite presence of God.

With prayer, we can live a life beyond our wildest dreams of achievement. Without it, we struggle, lose hope, become cynical, depressed, and apathetic. With God's touch, we truly awaken and become the faith-children of God. With prayer, we begin the endless journey of endless progress.

True Prayer

We've taken quite a journey in this book, but it's critical that we understand the essential foundation that makes it all possible: belief in the truths of The Universal Spiritual Way. Without these beliefs, it's not possible to attain the benefits of true prayer. We should remember that what we put in our minds either blocks or opens the way to God. *Our beliefs and our thoughts—not our feelings—are the doorway to God.*

First, you need to accept the experience of God that you're already having inside your very self. And when you accept what you're experiencing, you can firmly believe in God. But, you cannot stop there, because the type of God you envision—your concept of God—will affect the way that your mind experiences the REAL God.

God will certainly keep revealing himself to you, no matter what your misconceptions of him, but the sooner you let go of your preconceived notions of God, the sooner you'll begin to see the real God. In fact, this will be an eternal process since no human can ever have a perfect understanding of, or know all about God.

If we accept the fact that God is a loving, divine, eternal, perfect parent, that He gives us His absolute love, then we can begin the endless journey of God-discovery. And, once we accept that He is a loving, perfect being, we begin to trust Him completely as a child trusts a good earthly parent.

This foundation of trust will immediately help us to accept all other people as our sisters and brothers and remove our natural animal fear of them. Our lives will open into endless vistas of service and fulfillment, that is, if we pray based on the core truths of The Universal Spiritual Way.

> And when you become so readjusted to life within yourself, you become likewise readjusted to the universe; you have been born again—born of the spirit—and henceforth will your whole life become one of victorious accomplishment. Trouble will invigorate you; disappointment will spur you on; difficulties will challenge you; and obstacles will stimulate you. Arise . . . Say farewell to the life of cringing fear and fleeing cowardice. Hasten back to duty and live your life in the flesh as a (child) of God, a mortal dedicated to the ennobling service of man on earth and destined to the superb and eternal service of God in eternity.
>
> —Jesus, from *The Urantia Book*

When we pray with faith, with a sincere hunger for the truth and personal transformation so that we may give all to our loving Father, then, and only then, can we know a true spiritual life and its joys.

True prayer will transform your attitude toward life. True prayer is a complete surrender in sublime conversation to the matchless and all-encompassing, transformative embrace of the Father's spirit within. True prayer will change you completely and is the pathway to immersion in God—inner-worship.

When you ask God to help you be a better person, when you ask God to help others, when you open your heart to whatever answer He'll give, then you're ready for the sublime divine embrace of worship. When you tell God how much you appreciate and adore Him, when you give Him whatever love you have in total surrender, then you gain tremendous power and new ideals and insights.

Prayer is the ideal way to act on that power and insight to attain the new ideals, the stars that God reveals to you. Prayer is the ultimate and perfect transformative engine to help you change every part of yourself, to upstep your moral, religious, and ethical nature.

Prayer is the ultimate ingredient in that stupendous spiritual alchemy that you do with God. It should also be a spontaneous outpouring of communication with God, born of the consciousness of His presence.

True prayer is the breath of the soul.

Freedom from Human Limitations

Prayer doesn't change everything in the world, but it can release us from all human limitations so that *we're empowered* to change the world. Every one of us is faced with the basic limitations of being a human being. We have a variety of essential needs/hungers that reveal our limitations.

1. **Body.** All of us are physical creatures and subject to all the challenges of staying nourished and healthy, and all the limitations based on our bodies. We know that we face sickness, disability, disease, and death. Just contemplating these challenges could tempt anyone to give up hope.

   But, when we believe the truths of The Universal Spiritual Way and pray with faith, we realize that we're children of the Creator of the universe and can have an eternal future beyond all physical limitations. We can live forever after this first life.

2. **Prejudice and Assumptions.** Since we tend to initially think like animals, we tend to focus on only what we can see. We quickly build up opinions and prejudices that block out the truth from others and from God. We can be prisoners of our own pride and assumptions.

   Prayer is the only way to gain a release from our long-held intellectual prejudices and pride. Prayer is the gateway to experiences with God that will reveal the truth to us that will continually set us free. And, the most essential of these truths is that God is our Father and we're family.

3. **Material-Mindedness.** Materialism or material-mindedness is when we only think about material

things like possessions or even just surviving. We might not worship money, power, or things, but all of us can have the tendency to think mainly about only what we can see and what we need to obtain to survive the daily struggle.

Prayer helps us let go of this material-mindedness, this spiritual blindness. When we pray, we allow God to change our thoughts to help us see that all around us are family and that the highest satisfactions in life are found when we serve others. True religion is a religion of service to others.

4. **Incompleteness.** Each of us is mainly raw potential. Each of us has talents and a unique way of expressing and seeing life. But, we're just getting started; you and I are incomplete. We're certainly imperfect and have many gaps on the road to developing noble, eternal selves.

   Prayer gives us the contact we need from God to complete ourselves. Where we're incomplete, He gives completion. He may give us more than we can handle at times, but He'll give us everything we need to make ourselves more balanced and versatile to meet the challenge.

5. **Self-Focus.** Since we're essentially material beings, we need to first focus on self just to survive. Unfortunately, we often focus too much on ourselves and are insensitive to the needs or thoughts of others. When we focus so much on ourselves, our

development, our salvation, our progress, we begin to lose our ability to respond to the needs of others. And, if we continue, we eventually lose our ability to feel, to empathize, and this leads ultimately to selfishness and the disrespect and abuse of others.

When we come to God with sincere prayer, we transcend our self-focus to become focused on the needs of others. We feel total peace, assurance, and security that our loving Divine Father will meet all our true needs. We begin to collaborate more with others to gain group wisdom and achievements. Ultimately, this is the only way to a better world.

Everyone doesn't have to have the same opinions. We don't all have to think alike, but we can agree on the ultimate goals of so many of the challenges we face. Prayer is the only way to nourish ourselves to find this unity—through mutual dedication to the Father's will and the common experience of His spirit within.

Only truly spiritual countries can have peace with each other. The truest civilization is built on the ideals of a progressive spiritual and religious foundation. Each must eventually accept the essential truths of The Universal Spiritual Way.

6. **Death.** Everyone—sooner or later—will breathe their last breath. Some try to ignore this, others become depressed. But, to live life to the fullest, to do the best with the time we're given, we need to pray to find the

assurance that we can live an eternal life of endless achievement and joy.

Prayer is the only way to open ourselves to believe in this matchless promise from God.

7. **Finiteness.** And, how can any of us really forget that we're mostly finite, very limited human beings in a challenging world. When we face the immensity of life, the challenges, the joys, the disappointments, how can we have all the answers? How can we have the power to lead lives of joy and progress? How can we see beyond tomorrow toward the magnificent destiny God has designed for each of us?

   Prayer is the only way. Prayer allows us to be satisfied with making progress at our own speed and in actually helping God with His plan. Prayer reveals to us that each of us really has a unique place in this world, in this universe.

   Only you can fulfill God's destiny for you. Only you can help God with His incredible plan for universe development. Prayer will always show you the way beyond all limitations of your limited, finite self, into the unlimited, infinite future.

All of us have strong needs to meet the basic requirements for our bodies, to socialize with others, to grow, to achieve, to serve, and to love. But, unless we pray, we can never satisfy the most intense need of all—to have a relationship with God.

> The world is filled with hungry souls who famish in the very presence of the bread of life; men die searching for the very God who lives within them. Men seek for the treasures of the kingdom with yearning hearts and weary feet when they are all within the immediate grasp of living faith.
>
> —Jesus, from *The Urantia Book*

Prayer is truly the doorway to all. When we sincerely accept with all our hearts that we're children of God, we begin to use the faith-assurance from God to satisfy our hunger for truth and growth. Then we can ask God to change and empower us so that we will have even more faith—assurance, courage, ambition, and spiritual focus—to change the world.

Then, and only then, can we realize our destinies. Then and only then can we be supercharged.

Personal Prayer Transformations

Ideal prayer is a magic seed, a golden pebble thrown in a pond that sends remarkable, beneficial effects throughout our lives and those of others. When we face the world around and inside us, prayer is always the best reaction. In every inner and outer experience, prayer brings the divine essence for significant, unlimited personal transformation.

Instead of giving up when we hit barriers, we go forward again and again, selflessly, no matter what it takes. Instead of complaining about not being able to see the way ahead, instead of sitting down because we can't see around the corner, we strive on knowing that God can see around that corner and will give us just what we need, when we need it, in the way we need it, for as long as we need it.

When you pray with total faith, in that moment, you can know an incredible peace that allows you to totally trust that God will protect and nourish your spiritual self, a self that will ultimately go on for eternity. And when you have this peace, you can begin to know and express your real self every day in beautiful and inspiring living.

Our best example of perfect prayer is in the life of Jesus:

> Jesus brought to God, as a man of the realm, the greatest of all offerings: the consecration and dedication of his own will to the majestic service of doing the divine will. Jesus always and consistently interpreted religion wholly in terms of the Father's will. When you study the career of the Master, as concerns prayer or any other feature of the religious life, look not so much for what he taught as for what he did. Jesus never prayed as a religious duty. To him prayer was a sincere expression of spiritual attitude, a declaration of soul loyalty, a recital of personal devotion, an expression of thanksgiving, an avoidance of emotional tension, a prevention of conflict, an exaltation of intellection, an ennoblement of desire, a vindication of moral decision, an enrichment of thought, an invigoration of higher inclinations, a consecration of impulse, a clarification of viewpoint, a declaration of faith, a transcendental surrender of will, a sublime assertion of confidence, a revelation of courage, the proclamation of discovery, a confession of supreme devotion, the validation of consecration, a technique for the adjustment of difficulties, and the mighty mobilization of the combined soul powers to withstand

> all human tendencies toward selfishness, evil, and sin. He lived just such a life of prayerful consecration to the doing of his Father's will and ended his life triumphantly with just such a prayer. The secret of his unparalleled religious life was this consciousness of the presence of God; and he attained it by intelligent prayer and sincere worship—unbroken communion with God—and not by leadings, voices, visions, or extraordinary religious practices.
>
> —*The Urantia Book*

When we pray as Jesus of Nazareth prayed, we release a fountain of light and life that will transform our actions and our innermost selves. We'll be more kind, considerate, and powerful with our family, friends, and at work. When we use the inspiration and inner power we're given through prayer, there's no limit to how often we can live our spiritual destiny on earth.

True spirituality is the most powerful force to make this world a better place. The truly spiritual person nourished by prayer and inner-worship of God, can never really be defeated or ultimately discouraged. And, these are just the kind of people that are so badly needed right now in order to bring this world to an era of progress, knowledge, and wisdom.

All of these new leaders rely on prayer and the truths of The Universal Spiritual Way.

But, to transform the world, you need to be in the process of transforming yourself with prayer by following the Eternal Father's leading. You must be willing to trust God completely as a child trusts a good parent. You must surrender to the incredible process of growth.

The Adventure of Life Transformation

Every day, you and I have only one choice: Move forward or move backward. We're faced with needs and challenges shaped by our unique personalities, experiences, and choices. We're frequently faced with the need to choose to respond to the inner spiritual environment and the outer world.

The greatest gift God gives us is the miracle of self-conscious freewill. We know that we're alive, and we can make choices independently of the environment. We aren't puppets. We're the children of the Creator of the universe. And, when we actively seek and follow the guidance, the will of the Divine Father, we collaborate with God's spirit in that moment to become more than just human: We create our eternal selves.

> Your spirit nature—the jointly created soul—is a living growth, but the mind and morals of the individual are the soil from which these higher manifestations of human development and divine destiny must spring. The soil of the evolving soul is human and material, but the destiny of this combined creature of mind and spirit is spiritual and divine.
>
> —Jesus, paraphrased from *The Urantia Book*

But, the challenge is very large. Life on this rough planet requires us to work very hard to survive, to nourish our growth, to do the right thing for our family, friends, community, nations, all humankind, and the planet. And this means working so that the greatest number of people experience the greatest good for the greatest amount of time.

Prayer is ultimately the *greatest stimulus* for growth for all life's challenges. Profound prayer is the doorway to all the inspiration and power we need in order to follow the will of God in the perfect demonstration of the golden rule: Do unto others as you would have them do unto you. Treat people as you would like to be treated. Work for the true benefit of others as you would like them to work for your true benefit.

Treat people as you believe God would treat them, as His dear children. Practice divine fatherly love.

If you're serious about transforming yourself, you need to be serious about prayer. If you're serious about changing the world, you need to be serious about changing yourself.

But, take heart, even though you're imperfect and have many challenges (some that others will never understand), you have the ultimate doorway to the ultimate power. This power of the universe, the incredible love and energy from God, is yours for the asking. It's the doorway to eternity.

If you accept the spiritual experience that you're already having, and acknowledge the hunger to grow that is burning within your very soul, then you'll be able to begin to know God as a person and take the ultimate adventure, the destiny that He has for you.

You'll embark on an eternal journey of endless challenge, transformation, triumph, discovery, joy, and friendship. You'll be a true faith-child of God.

Remember, the most important thoughts you can have, the most effective way to keep the doorway to God open is to constantly think of the truths of The Universal Spiritual Way: You are a child of a loving, divine God. We're family. By using your faith you can have all your spiritual needs met and find a future of endless service to others, unlimited joy, and eternal life.

And, the most effective way to amplify those thoughts and find complete peace, assurance, security, confidence, self-forgetfulness, and power, is through prayer.

Prayer, inner-worship of God, and service to others is the passport to eternity.

> Believe and trust that as it is easy for you to breathe the air and live by it, or to eat and drink, so it is easy and even still easier for your faith to receive all spiritual gifts from the Lord. Prayer is the breathing of the soul: prayer is our spiritual food and drink.
>
> —John Sergieff of Kronstadt

Our loving Divine Father created you to take part in the stupendous unfolding of His divine universe plan. You have a unique place that no one can fill. You have a destiny and will be given everything you need to fulfill it. He has an incredible, wonderful, joyous life of unending joy and triumph for you.

Pray my Friend. Release the breath of your soul. Have faith. Find the life you were meant to live. Come home to your Divine Father. Talk to God each day. Supercharge your soul.

Spiritual Truths

Accepting God within will allow you to accept all people as your sisters and brothers and remove any fear of them.

True prayer completely transforms your attitudes, thinking, and actions.

Prayer helps us compensate for all human limitations.

True prayer continually renews and transforms you into an always-improving spiritual being.

Prayer is the most effective growth stimulus and the doorway to inner-worship and eternity.

Join My List, Ask a Question

Visit: FindMyNewLife.com

If you enjoyed this book, you'll be glad to know I've got another book that'll be released soon, and other projects after that. As soon as I have something I think you'd like, I'll send you an alert. Of course, you can get off the list at any time.

So, **please sign up today**. I'm looking forward to sharing more with you to help you on your journey. If you want to ask a question or make suggestions for a new offering, just let me know.

FindMyNewLife.com

Author's Message

It's really been a thrill to share this book with you, and I hope it's helped you on your spiritual journey. We're really all family of the same Creator, and I wish you the very best spiritual growth and personal success.

I know that whatever challenges you face, you can find peace and inspiration from God within. Things can get better. You can begin to live the life God meant for you.

You're unique and have a unique set of God-given gifts. You can find a better, more elevated life. It will bring you a new happiness and peace beyond your dreams: This is the life of real spiritual discovery with the real God.

I'll see you on the web and in my other projects.

All the best,

—Chris

About the Author

Who I Am

I'm a spiritual seeker—just like you—and do my best to follow my inner guidance. I have my struggles and challenges, but, I have complete faith that if I follow my inner light, things will be fine. God will take care of all my spiritual needs and give me the strength to face all my life challenges.

My mission is to write and speak to help people liberate themselves from everything that blocks or slows their spiritual awakening and progress.

Where I Live, What I've Done

I live on the East Coast of the United States with my wife and daughter and enjoy getting out to hike, bike ride, swim, and sail. This is my foundation and my biggest joy. And, I can't think of a more enjoyable thing to do than to climb a mountain.

I began my spiritual search in 1979 and have been involved in writing, speaking, and teaching since then. I actually published my first small book in 1992—*The Little Spiritual Answer Book*, and another small book in 1993—*God Without the Garbage* (both out of print).

I've worked as an elementary school teacher, high-tech salesman, a training designer, and—of course—a writer. I'm very excited about many new book projects to come.

Other Books by Christopher Lepine:

The Universal Spiritual Way:
A Complete Roadmap to a New Personal Life and a New Era for Humankind